VULNERABLE CHILDREN, VULNERABLE FAMILIES

THE SOCIAL CONSTRUCTION
OF CHILD ABUSE

VULNERABLE CHILDREN, VULNERABLE FAMILIES

THE SOCIAL CONSTRUCTION OF CHILD ABUSE

SUSAN JANKO

TEACHERS COLLEGE, COLUMBIA UNIVERSITY
NEW YORK AND LONDON

Published by Teachers College Press, 1234 Amsterdam Avenue
New York, NY 10027

Library of Congress Cataloging-in-Publication Data

Janko, Susan.
    Vulnerable children, vulnerable families : the social construction
of child abuse / Susan Janko.
        p.   cm.
    Includes bibliographical references and index.
    ISBN 0-8077-3306-7. — ISBN 0-8077-3305-9 (pbk.)
    1. Abused children — Services for — United States — Case studies.
2. Abusive parents — Behavior modification — United States — Case
studies.   3. Social work with families — United States — Case studies.
I. Title.
    HV6626.52.J36   1994
362.7′68′0973 — dc20   93-33595

ISBN 0-8077-3316-4
ISBN 0-8077-3315-6 (pbk.)

Printed on acid-free paper

Manufactured in the United States of America

98 97 96 95 94   8 7 6 5 4 3 2 1

CONTENTS

Acknowledgments vii

Chapter 1 1

INTRODUCTION

Determinants of Child Abuse
The Social Construction of Child Abuse
Parent Perspectives on Child Abuse
Data Collection

Chapter 2 14

VULNERABLE CHILDREN, VULNERABLE FAMILIES

Three Parents' Stories
Family Histories

Chapter 3 31

CHILD PROTECTIVE SERVICES — PREVENTION
AND INTERVENTION

Substantiating Child Maltreatment
Legal Intervention
The Parenting Program
Parents' Impressions of the Parenting Program: Early Optimism

Chapter 4 50

IN THE SYSTEM

The Perpetuation of Child Maltreatment
Family Theory
The Crime of Poverty
In The Child's Best Interest
The Functions of Child Protective Services
Parents and CPS: Them and Us
Things Must Fall Apart

Chapter 5. 75

SUPPORTING, REPARENTING, AND EMPOWERING

Parent and Professional Relationships
Supporting Families by Empowering Parents
Coming Full Circle: Preventing Maltreatment
"These Kids Do Not Come with Parenting Manuals"
Intervention in the Contexts of Family and Community

Chapter 6. 101

GETTING OUT OF THE SYSTEM

The Importance of Appearing Earnest
No Way Out
Conclusions: Making Sense of Nonsense
Changing the System

Chapter 7. 122

AFTERWORD: REFLECTIONS ON CHANGE

The Why of Change
The How of Change
Parents and Families Revisited

Appendix. 137

METHODS

A Field Study Approach
A Grounded Theory Approach
Quality Assurance in Qualitative Research
Adopting the Role of Researcher

References. 157

Index. 163

About the Author. 168

ACKNOWLEDGMENTS

I would like to express my sincere gratitude to Dianne Ferguson for her clear thinking, kind support, and gentle prodding; to Diane Bricker for offering professional challenges and helping me to meet them; to Peggy Veltman, Gene Edgar, and Mary Carr for reading early drafts, conversations that challenged and shaped my thinking, sharing family stories, and the inspiration of professional behavior that exhibits a strong and unwavering sense of purpose; and especially to Christopher Haugen and Kathrin Holt for helping me make family stories, seek balance, and find meaning. Most of all, I am grateful for the generous gifts of the unnamed colleagues, cherished friends, and families in the Parenting Program.

Chapter 1

Introduction

There appears to be an epidemic of child abuse in America. Reported incidents of child abuse and neglect increased 225% from 1976 to 1987 (Alsop, 1990), and more than 10% of parents in a national survey reported that they engaged in "severe violent acts" against their children during the previous year (Strauss & Gelles, 1986). As many as 62% of girls and 31% of boys are suspected to have experienced sexual abuse during childhood (Dubowitz, 1986).

Child abuse was rarely acknowledged or discussed a generation ago (Cichetti & Carlson, 1989). During the 1990s, however, child abuse is reported in the morning newspaper; it is the stuff of television talk shows, and stories about child abuse appear frequently in popular periodicals such as *Newsweek, Glamour, Ladies Home Journal, McCalls,* and *Vanity Fair* — even *Seventeen* and *Rolling Stone.* A sensational spectrum of images is conveyed by the media — ranging from Oprah Winfrey's disclosure of having experienced abuse and allegations that Woody Allen sexually molested his 7-year-old daughter (Adler et al., 1992) to the testimonials of people who survived satanic cults (Smith and Pazder, 1989) and adults remembering "with mounting horror" the sexual molestation they suffered as children by their trusted parish priest (Woodward, 1991, p. 60).

What does the phrase "child abuse" signify to our society? To many it conjures images of victimized children and sadistic adults, and evokes sympathy for child victims as well as condemnation of adult perpetrators. Lurid stories reported in periodicals and on radio or television about ritualistic beatings, sexual molestation, torture, and starvation of young children influence our understanding of child abuse and appeal to our voyeurism, regardless of their verity. Media coverage of the most extreme cases of abuse and neglect masks the complex realities of most incidents of child maltreatment. Our misperceptions about child abuse are evident in our response to the problem. We criticize agencies designed to protect children for allowing children to remain in situations where they are mistreated or intervening only after children have been harmed. Simultaneously we accuse those agencies of violating the rights of parents suspected of maltreating their children and of falsely accus-

1

ing others. Despite the apparent prevalence of child maltreatment, society's increased attention to the problem, and the number of programs that exist to address the problem, the issue of child abuse remains surrounded by questions and uncertainty. Popular portrayals of child mistreatment represent only partial truths about the problem (Pelton, 1985).

DETERMINANTS OF CHILD ABUSE

In 1975, Arnold Sameroff and Michael Chandler published "Reproductive Risk and the Continuum of Caretaking Casualty," which stressed the important influence that transactions between the developing child and the caretaking environment have on developmental outcomes of children and incidents of child maltreatment. Since that time, at least in theory if not in practice, the mutuality of the contributions of children and their caretakers within the environmental contexts of social stress and support has been viewed as significant in understanding and impacting parent-child relationships. Theoretical and philosophical underpinnings of intervention for child mistreatment have shifted the focus from the child or parent to the family as a unit; however, popular beliefs about child abuse and current practices of child protective services continue to focus almost exclusively on the abusive parent and ignore the influence of child characteristics and the environment on incidents of abuse (Wolfe, 1985).

Parental characteristics associated with abuse and neglect have been described as both personal/psychological and ontogenic (Belsky & Vondra, 1989). Examples of personal/psychological characteristics attributed to abusive parents include maternal apathy, aggression, chronic depression, personality disorders, and cognitive impairments (Meier & Sloan, 1984). Ontogenic characteristics, those that reflect the personal developmental histories of parents labeled abusive and contribute to the social, cognitive, and affective processes that influence caregiving relationships, include experiences of being maltreated as a child, family conflict and resolution, and parenting histories (Pianta, Egeland, & Erickson, 1989).

Whereas children were at one time believed to be products of their physical and social environments in combination with their underlying genetic constitutions, they are now viewed as active agents in the complex transactions that contribute to developmental structures and behavioral outcomes. There is evidence that certain behavioral and developmental characteristics may predispose them to maltreatment. Child characteristics believed to be associated with vulnerability to maltreatment include relatively permanent or chronic conditions such as developmental disabilities, medical fragility, and temperament traits, as well as more transitory or situational characteristics such as prematurity, low birth weight, discipline problems, sexual acting out, or poor performance in school (Meier & Sloan, 1984).

Child and parent characteristics, although important to understand child maltreatment, are not sufficient to explain the phenomenon. Discrete examination of child and parent characteristics belies such characteristics' interdependence in influencing incidents of child maltreatment and ignores the role of the environments in which parent and child development occur. The environment, particularly the culturally determined behaviors, beliefs, and attitudes that constitute institutional customs and practices, provides a medium that "pulls the hair trigger of intrinsic development" (Bowman, 1992, p. 101). Characteristics of the environment related to abuse and neglect may be viewed in terms of whether they add elements of stress or support to child-caregiver relationships, such as having adequate money, food, housing, health care, and available adults to share caregiving responsibilities. These stresses and supports occur at all levels—within family relationships, through community resources, and in response to social policies and program funding that influence the availability of resources to families and communities. Environmental stress and lack of support impact the very characteristics associated with the high-risk status of children and negative child outcomes, as evidenced in the relationship between poverty and infant morbidity.

The synergetic relationship between the developing child and the caregiving and social environments is apparent in the all too frequent scenario of the pregnant adolescent who is homeless, smokes cigarettes, and uses multiple drugs throughout her pregnancy, receives no prenatal care, and delivers a premature, low birth-weight and drug-affected infant who is immediately removed from her mother's care by CPS. The young mother learns to parent her vulnerable, challenging baby in the context of brief weekly visits at the CPS office while she leads the disorienting life of one who does not have the psychological and emotional grounding that comes from reliable family and friends, consistent meals, a bed to sleep in, and one's belongings accessible and safe. It is to this developing parent that this baby, who in her young life has experienced illness and a series of abruptly severed relationships with her biological and foster care families, will return to live out her life.

It is seductive to believe that one need only intervene with the guilty parent to address abuse and neglect, but that approach ignores our knowledge of the powerful roles of parent-child relationships, families, communities, and society in the dynamics of child maltreatment.

THE SOCIAL CONSTRUCTION OF CHILD ABUSE

The ways in which society understands and defines child maltreatment are closely linked to the ways the child welfare system interprets and responds to the legal definition of child maltreatment. The status children hold in relation to families and society, and the societal values and interpretations of what constitutes appropriate and inappropriate parenting differ from community to community (Garbarino, 1990). Because of the influence of societal values on the definition and recognition of certain behaviors, conditions, and situations as abusive, and the influence of societal values and social policies on those behaviors, conditions, and situations, the prevalence of child maltreatment may appear to change, although the actual caregiving situations children encounter are relatively unchanged (Pelton, 1990). Therefore, the recent and dramatic increase in the number of reported cases of child maltreatment may indicate a real increase in the prevalence of child maltreatment, or it may result from an increased societal response to a perceived social crisis. Moreover, the social crisis may be real enough, but the perception that the inadequate care experienced by so many children in our country can be described most accurately as child abuse and that the responsibility for providing care lies solely, or primarily, with their parents (and most often with their mothers) is questionable. How do our perceptions and definitions of maltreatment influence our responses and interventions?

The first legal definitions of abuse and neglect in our country were developed for the purpose of designating situations in which public authorities had the right to intervene on behalf of children (Giovannoni, 1989). Legal mandates focused on the inadequacies of parents rather than the condition of children and identified three categories of parental failure: "(1) endangering the morals of their children; (2) exhibiting morally reprehensible behavior themselves; and (3) endangering the life and health of children" (McCrea, 1910 in Giovannoni, 1989). Intervention, once parental failure was identified, frequently consisted of removal of the child from the abusing family.

In the late 1800s, the Society for the Prevention of Cruelty to Children (SPCC) was organized by the leadership of the Society for the Prevention of Cruelty to Animals in response to the discovery of the beating and starvation of an 8-year-old child by her adoptive parents.

At the time, there were no laws prohibiting child maltreatment and the New York City police would not intervene, so the SPCC advocated on the child's behalf (Zigler & Hall, 1989). Largely as a result of the work of the SPCC, child abuse came to be seen as a distinct social problem, and SPCC chapters functioned as quasi law enforcement agencies, investigating reports of abuse, presenting evidence in court, and advising the court on dispositions (Giovannoni, 1989). Although law enforcement activities were performed in conjunction with social services by the SPCC in the early 1900s, as juvenile court systems were established and the field of social work became professionalized and distinct from the legal system, a preventive orientation to the problem of child maltreatment evolved (Giovannoni, 1989).

Some argue that there has been a preventive orientation to child maltreatment in rhetoric only, and the focus of the child welfare system and allocation of resources for child welfare have been and continue to be used for the purpose of investigating families and removing their children (Pelton, 1990). This policy of intervention tends toward law enforcement rather than prevention or remediation of abuse and neglect, and it appears to be guided by a belief that when a child's welfare is compromised, the responsibility lies primarily with the child's parent. According to this logic, children who have been maltreated will fare better if removed from their families.

Removal of children from their homes and placement in foster care or institutional care in response to a perceived social crisis has a long history in our country, according to Pelton (1990):

> In the 1850s, Charles Loring Brace and his New York Children's Aid Society was apparently successful in making the case that the immigrant children who were wandering the streets of New York City's poorest neighborhoods, unsupervised and not being educated, needed to be placed in foster homes "out West." His society raised money enough to eventually place tens of thousands of children, and his example stimulated a proliferation of child-placing agencies (pp. 19–20).

A century later, the foster care population doubled during the 1960s and 1970s when Kempe and his colleagues identified a "battered child syndrome" (Kempe, Silverman, Steele, Droegemueller, & Silver, 1962). "The social construction of child abuse as a social problem of 'epidemic' proportions served to drive the explosion in foster care placements, fueled by new child abuse and neglect reporting laws, public awareness campaigns, and increased funding for social services, much of which was used for foster care" (Pelton, 1990).

Pelton (1990) believes the social interventions we use and the resources we allocate are critical factors in determining the number of children in foster care. Monetary resources allocated for removal and foster care placement were triple those allocated for therapeutic family intervention during 1989 (Pelton, 1990). The number and type of interventions available and resources to pay for them are in turn driven by our perceptions of social crises. Children in foster care are primarily "from families most deeply submerged in poverty" according to Pelton (p. 20). During the 1850s, uneducated children of immigrants were the focus of concern of child welfare. During the 1960s and 1970s, "battered" children were the focus, and during the 1980s and 1990s, the focus shifted to children of parents who abuse drugs and alcohol, have mental illness or disabilities, or are homeless—those on the fringes of our society. The common denominators among the changing foci of concern across time are minority status and poverty.

Gelles' (1977, cited in Giovannoni, 1989) survey of 157 physicians indicated that the socioeconomic status and ethnicity of caregivers and the severity of the child's injuries interacted in their effect on physicians' recognition of child maltreatment. Professionals are more likely to recognize and label behavior as "abusive" if parents are poor or of color than if they are middle class and white. Although child abuse and neglect are present in all ethnic groups and across socioeconomic levels, reports of abuse and neglect occur predominantly in families of low socioeconomic status (Gil, 1970; Pelton, 1985). Families in poverty are greatly overrepresented in the child welfare system.

Poverty, while having a real influence on children's health, development, and caregiving environments, has no apparent relationship with foster care population trends. Rather, the reasons for removal of children from their homes change according to society's perceptions about some problem or issue (Pelton, 1990). The total number of removals of children seems to be contingent upon the perceived importance by society of those problems or issues, the resources made available to child welfare agencies for investigation of alleged incidents of maltreatment, removal of children, and placement in foster care, and the simplistic notion that foster care or adoption are antidotes to child maltreatment.

The process of distinguishing between the normal and the pathological is dynamic, as Moynihan (1993) points out, and society's definitions of deviance can be adjusted upwards or downwards. These adjustments in society's perceptions about what does or does not constitute a problem result in a corresponding change in the intensity or magnitude with which society deals with the perceived problem regardless of whether there is a real increase or decrease in the prevalence of or change in the characteristics of the problem. This discussion of societal definitions of and responses to deviance is not merely academic. It is within the context of society and in relation to these convoluted definitions that the drama of involvement with the CPS system is played out by real children and families.

PARENT PERSPECTIVES ON CHILD ABUSE

This book is about parents who were alleged by a state child welfare system to have abused their children. It attempts to portray the ways in which child maltreatment by parents identified as abusive is defined, and it tells the story of three parents and families in particular. This book is based on a study I conducted in an intervention program for maltreated children called the "Parenting Program" that was co-sponsored by a state CPS agency and a nonprofit, therapeutic preschool program that operated from a community church. I conceived the idea of conducting the study during a time when I directed the therapeutic preschool program and co-directed the Parenting Program, but I began the study after I left those positions. The study was driven by my dissatisfaction with the child welfare system, as well as my desire to understand more about child maltreatment and families identified as abusive than available theories, models, and prevailing characterizations allowed.

When I directed the program I frequently encountered situations that appeared contradictory. The parents in the program were characterized by colleagues as deviant, yet in my view, most parents seemed more like me than different from me. Visitors to the program echoed my impressions and expressed surprise that the children looked like "regular" children and the parents like "regular" parents. I felt uncomfortable as I observed my colleagues establishing what seemed to be adversarial relationships with the parents, and I had difficulty reconciling the frequently encountered view of these parents as malevolent with my own observations of them. I was aware that many of the parents had themselves been abused as children and had never received treatment. When they made passage into parenthood, unprepared to parent and frequently still children themselves, they came to be viewed as perpetrators warranting prosecution rather than victims needing support.

In addition, issues related to poverty frequently overshadowed specific concerns about parenting. Parents demonstrated competent parenting skills during class, but were unable to provide shelter, clothing, food, and medical care for their children. The inconsistency with which individual cases were treated by CPS added to the confusion. While some parents awaited the return of their children from foster care until they obtained jobs, others were instructed by caseworkers not to work because their children needed them at home. For many parents, income from Aid to Families with Dependent Children (AFDC, or "welfare checks") or from minimum wage jobs as dishwashers or fast food clerks were insufficient to acquire or maintain housing, and the number of families in the program who were homeless steadily increased. Parenting issues became secondary to issues of daily survival.

I often felt frustrated and angry with a child welfare system that seemed more reactive to crises than responsive to what I believed to be children and families' real need for food, shelter, and respite. A mother once told me she had telephoned CPS in tears and asked for help, afraid she would physically harm her children. An anonymous voice over the phone told her CPS could not do anything until her children had already been hurt.

Some parents appeared to do an adequate job of parenting while they attended the program, yet their children remained in foster care. At other times, I observed children returned to homes that I considered too dangerous to send staff to to conduct home visits. The basis for decisions about removal of children from their homes seemed unclear, and the outcomes of those decisions were frustrating and discouraging.

Ann, a parent in the program and one of the key figures in this book, told me, "Child Protective Services is a bureaucracy. Their response to a complaint is, 'It's policy.' Nobody wants to take the time to see what works." Ann believed that someone ought to conduct a survey to discover what people thought. She believed that if a number of people thought the policies were bad, they could be changed. The study and this book are my attempt to take the time to see what works and what does not work, to listen to the thoughts and experiences of people involved with the system of child welfare—staff, and especially parents. Like Ann, I believe the child welfare system does not meet its stated goals and purposes. Moreover, it is my opinion that the child welfare system's identification of parents who live in poverty as neglectful and abusive is discriminatory and contributes to the problems and misconceptions associated with child abuse. I believe much can be learned from families who experience the CPS system firsthand, and that it is important that they have a voice. I designed and conducted this study in a way that allows the parents' views to predominate. At the same time, it is important to remember that the important voices of their children are missing.

It is a painful enterprise to learn and write about the lives of families in such truly desperate circumstances, and in large part, the demoralization — and at times despair — I felt as I collected data shaped the direction of the study. As the study neared completion and my feelings of hopelessness grew, I felt compelled to do more than describe the problems experienced by the families and staff, and I questioned parents and professionals about their thoughts on how the child welfare system should change. Their ideas and optimism are incorporated in Chapter 6.

DATA COLLECTION

The book is organized in a way that I hope will allow a progressive awareness of some issues surrounding child maltreatment. Chapters are arranged in a sequence similar to the order in which data were collected. The initial chapters introduce parents and staff and describe the Parenting Program, the incidents that precipitated families' involvement with CPS, investigations of alleged child maltreatment, and parents' and families' histories. Subsequent chapters describe parents' experiences after having entered the child welfare system, their attempts to exit the system, and the ways decisions were made concerning the return of children, case closure, and termination of parental rights. Parents' and staff's reactions to the study and descriptions of how families fared after exiting the program are included at the end of the book, along with an analysis of and recommendations for changing the system. This is followed by an Appendix detailing the methodology of the study.

As I collected data I was struck by the frequent, momentous events and changes that occurred in the lives of these families. Along with descriptions of ways families entered and exited the child welfare system and parents' perceptions of the system, the events that occurred during the study are incorporated in the chapters. I attempt to chronicle these events in order to capture the mercurial lives of the families in the program while maintaining a focus on more global issues.

Consistent with the purpose of the study and this book — to discover parents' perspectives of child maltreatment and the services they received as a result of that label — I observed parents identified as abusive by CPS along with their children and the Parenting Program staff, during weekly intervention sessions, 1 day each week, for a period of 4 months. Observations lasted approximately 5 hours each day that intervention sessions were held. Weekly observations included staff planning meetings prior to the sessions, the intervention sessions, and the "debriefing" meetings that followed each intervention session and allowed the program staff to discuss programmatic issues and review the progress of the families with whom they worked.

In addition to observations of families and staff during intervention, quantitative data about the demographics and characteristics of 55 parents and their children, who were enrolled in the program during the year I conducted the study, were collected in order to provide a broader, although more superficial, view of all of the families in the program. Twenty of those families were enrolled in the program during the time I conducted participant observations and are represented in the narrative, but my research focused on three families in particular. The parents of the three families were interviewed between 3 and 7 times each, and conversations occurred weekly throughout the initial 4-month period of data collection. Informal conversations were recorded in the form of field notes. Formal interviews usually lasted about 1½ hours and occurred during visits outside the program. Some visits lasted as little as 3 hours, others lasted as long as 5 hours. I spent time with families in restaurants, parks, movie theaters, welfare offices, and discount stores. I watched the parents practice their parenting skills when their children were cooperative, affectionate, and compliant, and when they were oppositional, challenging, and angry. After I moved from the city in which the study was conducted, I corresponded with one parent through letters and frequent, extended long distance telephone calls.

When the majority of the interviews with parents were complete, I interviewed a number of staff members in the intervention program regarding topics that had been raised by the parents during earlier conversations and interviews. Finally, I solicited and interviewed knowledgeable staff members who were affiliated with CPS to clarify questions I had about procedures and policies. None of the CPS workers affiliated with the Parenting Program consented to participate in the study, with the exception of Georgia, the program co-director.

The staff members were eager to talk and frequently asked when I would interview them. Because I was familiar and viewed as an insider, I think I was privy to information from staff that might not have been shared as readily if I had been an outsider. My previous role as a staff member also presented disadvantages, however. At the beginning of the study, staff invited my opinions and advice. When I declined to respond, they questioned when I would finish collecting data. Evidence that I did a good job of not offering opinions occurred near the end of the study when a staff member commented that "the data collector finally came out of her shell" and staff applauded after I uttered an expletive about an emotionally charged and controversial situation with a family. For most staff and parents, I believe I was seen as someone other than program staff.

The parents were slow to talk initially. I recall a palpable silence one afternoon when we gathered in a large meeting room in the church that housed the Parenting Program. I described the study to the parents enrolled in the program, told them that I wanted to learn their experiences and views, and invited their participation. After waiting a long, quiet spell for a comment or question, I assured families, who sat looking forward with arms crossed, that I was not from CPS, and I explained how I would not divulge their identities or share any information about them with anyone from the Parenting Program or CPS.[1] However, as part of obtaining informed consent, I communicated one exception to that assurance. Upon the insistence of the committee at the university that oversaw research and insured the protection of human subjects, I informed parents verbally and in writing that I was bound to report any abuse I discovered during my research and that my records could be subpoenaed to court. Those warnings probably did not enhance my trustworthiness in their eyes; however, after observing from a distance for some weeks, several parents eventually approached me.

Two of the three parents whose stories predominate in this book had attended the intervention program prior to my study, so I was familiar to them although we were not acquainted. Most other parents knew me as a university student working on a research project and never appeared to think of me as part of the program. Not all of the parents in the program talked about their experiences in detail or freely shared their opinions, but most stopped by occasionally to ask how "the book" was going. The two parents who knew me before I began my research willingly talked to me when I requested interviews, but Ann, the parent who proved to be the most responsive informant and my greatest resource for information, did not know me prior to the study. Although one story may be as important as the next, I will always wonder why some parents talked and others did not. I have a hunch that if I had collected data in the program for a period longer than 4 months, more parents would have shared information and views. On

---

[1] All of the names of people, programs, and locations have been changed to protect the privacy of those involved.

the other hand, it was difficult listening to the stories of the families' tragic, seemingly hopeless lives, and I frequently felt overwhelmed with sadness and a sense of powerlessness. I am not certain that I really desired or could have managed to interview more parents. Temporal and emotional resources imposed restrictions.

My professional training in the fields of psychology and early childhood special education did not prepare me for the realities of the children's and families' lives I encountered or the feelings of professional inadequacy I experienced during this study. I first became involved with high-risk children and families through my interest in the language development of children living in poverty. I was trained to believe in the power of the clinical skills I had acquired to work with children and families, and I felt confident in their application and optimistic about the outcomes I could effect. This research has shaken my beliefs about the efficacy of intervention as it is commonly understood and promoted, and it has forced me to think about early intervention in very different and much broader ways. The experiences in the lives of the families I met have resulted in significant changes in my life and the way I make sense of the world.

I feel indebted to the parents and staff who generously gave their time and eloquently communicated their feelings, ideas, and experiences. People opened their homes and shared their confidences. Ann, a parent who had perpetual problems scraping together enough money for groceries each month, wanted to give me a gold pendant with a small diamond embedded in it — a possession from earlier, better times. She expressed gratitude too many times to recount for my willingness to spend time with her and listen to her. I attempted to explain how our conversations benefited me and to express my thanks, but she told me she never really understood how she could be helping me. Another parent told a staff member that I was her "best friend." As my research progressed, my knowledge about the personal lives of the families and their views of the child welfare system increased. Sometimes I was pleasantly surprised; at other times I became aware of things I would rather not have known. Ignorance is, as they say, bliss — or at least innocence. As a result of the three women who shared their stories with me, I will never again view families, society, or my profession in the same way, and for that I am both very sad and very grateful.

Agar (1980) has said that "ethnography is really quite an arrogant enterprise" (p. 41). If I was arrogant at the outset of this endeavor, I felt humbled by its end. Any portrayal of real people and real situations, whether that portrayal is numeric, photographic, or descriptive, is superficial. This study provides a glance at a few families who allowed their privacy to be invaded, in one geographical area of the country, in one intervention program, for one brief period of time. Despite my earnest efforts, this book presents a crude representation of the families and the Parenting Program. My greatest concern is that I have accurately portrayed the information I gathered from the families and program staff. My efforts toward that goal are explained in an Appendix, which contains a description of the research methods I used to conduct the study, and the final chapter of the study, which contains the reactions of the families and Parenting Program staff to the study.

With that brief introduction, this is how three parents came to be known as abusive by a CPS system, what happened to them and their children after they entered that system, and how they survived it and made sense of it.

CHAPTER 2

VULNERABLE CHILDREN,
VULNERABLE FAMILIES

Home is the place where, when you have to go there,
They have to take you in.
— Robert Frost, "The Death of the Hired Hand"

In some ways it is difficult to describe the families in the program. As I have already said, most of the parents seemed more like me than different from me. But it is also true that during the 15-year period during which I worked with young children with disabilities and their families, I had never before encountered such situations as a fist fight between a mother and her sister outside my classroom doors, the need to arrange for children in my classroom to place a long distance call to speak to their father in prison, or having to call a colleague to warn her that a parent who was served by both our programs had threatened to burn down her house.

Yet I could not say that those parents were typical of all of the parents in the program. Each parent and each child had unique characteristics and reasons for being there. Of the 55 parents enrolled in the Parenting Program during the 12 months I collected data there, 25 were single, and 30 were married. The majority were between 20 and 30 years of age, although many had been adolescent parents. Some had previously been involved with Child Protective Services; others were involved with CPS for the first time. Most parents, 37 of the 55 parents enrolled, had been ordered by the court to attend the Parenting Program. These descriptions of marital status and previous involvement with CPS tell us something about the parents in the program, but they do little to elucidate the reasons parents and families became involved with Child Protective Services.

THREE PARENTS' STORIES

This chapter contains my impressions of three of the parents during the time of our first meeting, and it tells the stories they shared with me about their involvement with Child Protective Services. It is important to note that the voices of the three women featured in this book, while providing insight about parenting from the perspectives of single women raising children alone, do not portray the perspectives of the individual children in their families or their families as a unit.

Jean

Jean was 22 years of age and had long, medium blonde hair, green eyes, and a pretty face, unmasked by makeup, that looked clean and shiny like her hair. Petite in stature and bone structure, she was usually smiling, and if you looked at her or spoke to her when she wasn't smiling, she responded immediately with a smile that was spontaneous and joyful, although mostly toothless.

Jean described her five children as "little stair steps" because of the closeness in their ages and sizes. They ranged in age from 10 months to 7 years and to varying degrees looked like Jean. All had some shade of blonde hair, some curly, some straight like Jean's, and all were attractive. Her oldest daughter was born when Jean was 14, a second daughter when she was 16, a son at 18, a daughter at 20, and a fourth daughter, her fifth child, was born by the time Jean was 21. Jean seemed older than her 22 years and said she felt older too.

None of the three different fathers of the children were available to the family on a regular basis. One of the fathers called his daughter on her sixth birthday. It was the second time in her life the child had spoken to him. One of the father's whereabouts was unknown, and another had recently been released from jail after serving 18 months for driving with a revoked license.

Two years before I met Jean, her four children had been taken into custody by CPS. At the time, her youngest child was 4 months old and she was pregnant with her fifth child. She and her children lived in a "disgusting" mobile home with Jean's mother and older brother, who were alone and without money since her father's death. Jean, as she told the circumstances of her children's removal by CPS, acknowledged responsibility — with a few disclaimers.

> *Jean*: The kids' dad was in jail and I was too busy trying to get up there to see him to give him money, to do the things he wanted me to do. I totally ignored the kids. I left them with babysitters. They'd hardly ever see me. Ned was molesting my oldest daughter.
> *Susan*: Who's Ned?

Jean: [He's] my brother, my oldest brother. And she was trying to tell me. And I was [saying], 'Oh, you're just being a bad child again,' and I'd slap her and stuff. When I look back on it, I can see everything—every attempt she [made] to tell me, and she did try to tell me. I mean, once she even came right out and said it, and I thought she was lying. I didn't pay attention. He discredited her so much to me, I just thought she was the biggest brat on the face of the earth.

Susan: You mean your brother discredited her?

Jean: Yeah. And . . . all kids lie, but my daughter is about the one child of mine that rarely ever lies. Everything is precisely to the point, and she tries to be as honest as possible. She told her teacher about it, and CPS removed her from school.

Susan: Was she about 6 then?

Jean: She was just a little over 6.

Susan: And your next daughter must have been, what, about 4?

Jean: Yeah, she was. She was about 4½. And then my son was almost 2, and my youngest daughter was 4 months.

Susan: Did they remove all the kids?

Jean: Yeah. They removed them all because when they [came to] remove the kids, I [hadn't] cleaned the house, nothing. There were piles of garbage in each corner. I didn't do dishes. I hardly had any food for the kids. All their clothes were dirty.

Susan: Were you using drugs?

Jean: No. I never used drugs. But I did just about every other thing that you can think of that was really terrible.

During a later interview, Jean's story changed slightly. She said she knew her brother was sexually abusing both her daughters a week before the children were removed, but because her mother and brother had nowhere else to go, she let them live in a car parked beside her mobile home. Jean said that her brother gained entry to her mobile home through her front door, which couldn't be locked. When I asked Jean about her childcare arrangements, she told me she had a "good babysitter" for her children. Her 28-year-old brother found sufficient time when her children were unattended to sexually assault her 4- and 6-year-old daughters, however.

Jean said she never realized how much her children meant to her until they were taken from her by Child Protective Services—before that she had thought of them as little dolls you dressed up and took out and afterward put up on a shelf. According to Jean, there was a striking change in her ideas about parenting after Child Protective Services intervened in her life. If that is so, it is impossible to determine from this interview because Jean neglects to mention what happened to her children, where they were placed, if they remained together, and how they fared.

Jean: The first couple of months, boy, I went cuckoo.

Susan: What happened during that time?

Jean: I don't know. To tell you the truth, I really don't know. I don't remember. I know they were taken away. I know I freaked. I remember I went to see them every Tuesday. Well, actually it was every Monday. I remember I went to see them, and I did everything CPS wanted me to do.

Susan: What kinds of things did they want you to do?

Jean: Then it was just visitation. And I tried to find a house.

Susan: Were you homeless?

Jean: Yeah. I was homeless for 6 months. And I was pregnant.

Susan: Where did you stay?

Jean: I cannot — I remember going to see the kids, but I don't remember much of nothing else. And that's how much of a shock I went through. The kids' dad's mom said I stayed with her. And I'm sure I did, because what else was I going to do? I really — it's just all really foggy to me what I did the first couple of months.

Susan: Did you know who CPS was?

Jean: Not at the time.

Susan: So they were never involved with your family?

Jean: No. They should have been, but no, they weren't. It was all very new to me. Very new. At first I thought, 'You fuckers, you took my kids. Those are my kids.' Then after they explained to me what was going on, and the circumstances and stuff, and the depth of all this, I said, "Okay." I walked out of there and I felt really secure about where they're at.

Susan: Who did you talk to?

Jean: My caseworker. She is a doll.

Susan: What did she say to make you feel secure? Most parents said they didn't know what was going on and nobody would tell them anything.

Jean: Oh, my caseworker explained everything in detail to me. She even explained the court proceedings, and we sat there for a good two hours talking. She told me that Ned had been raping my daughters and that they had doctors' reports stating that it was true, that my oldest daughter had been injured and stuff. The house wasn't in living condition.

It was bad. It seemed like a big nightmare to me. All of a sudden I could feel all the [old] anger back and [I was] wishing that someone would have protected me when I was little. And I felt, well, my kids feel secure now. Now it's time for me to take care of [my brother]. And I went down on the mall and I shoved him — literally. I don't know where I got the strength, but I hurt him bad. This guy looks like an ape. He weighs 260 pounds.

Susan: And you're what — about 5′2″?

Jean: I'm 5′, and I weigh 93 pounds. He was in Woolworth's restaurant, and I just literally picked him up and shoved him on the table, and I'm screaming and slapping him and stuff, saying, "You fucking child molester." And everybody's yelling, "Yeah, yeah." There were two guys, and they were real cute, and I told them, "Shut up. I don't want no applause, no nothing." I was taking care of what I had to take care of. And my mom — I don't agree with the way my mom raised me or the way she acted, but she was still my mom, I had to give [her] credit. And she got in the way, in between us. Wrong thing to do. I slammed into a couple of tables. They called the cops on me, and the cops hauled me out of there, and they told me, they said, "What's going on?" and I told them what [was] going on. They said, "You should stay away from him." I said, "I'm going to kill the fucker. Watch me, I'll kill him. In cold blood, dead." And the cop said, "Miss Kemp, is that a threat?" I said, "You take it as you want it, but mark my word."

And so they put a restraining order on me. I mean really. [What I did] was stupid, but I think [I did] it [because of] all the anger [in] me and [because of what happened to] my kids. I just lost it. And I stayed lost for 4 months.

Despite the life Jean had led, she appeared to me to be undaunted. She seemed to go blithely on her way, taking things in stride that might seem tragic to others. As I observed her over time and learned some of her history, I was left with the impression that Jean's life stretched ahead and behind in a parade of calamities, each one unquestioned and unchallenged by her. She seemed to march along with the parade. I projected that after everything Jean had experienced during her life, she must have believed that chaos and tragedy were ordinary, daily life events — or perhaps she just reframed the truth about the events in her life so that her reality was easier to live with.

It seemed different for Ann. Whereas Jean appeared to live life without a care, Ann seemed to stoop under the weight of life's burdens.

Ann

Ann was a 29-year-old woman with thick, dark hair that hung in waves beneath her shoulders. It was always clean and the color was in stark contrast with her fair, clear complexion. Ann was fairly tall and athletic looking. Her face held a dour expression and her shoulders typically hunched forward as if she carried the weight of the world. This posture and scowl effectively masked a quick sense of humor and an intelligence that I imagine few people recognized or persevered long enough to discover. Ann frequently lacked charm and social grace, and more than once I felt embarrassed standing by as she verbally challenged a waitress, clerk, or ticket taker.

I suppose Ann's demeanor reflected the toll her life had taken upon her. During the ten months immediately following Ann's involvement with CPS, she had been hospitalized for depression, had twice had her son abruptly removed and placed in foster care, had been alone and homeless, and had divorced and given up custody of her son to her husband, then reunited with her husband, Mike. Ann once told me, "I think I've lost what normal is. I don't think I remember what it is anymore. I really don't remember what it's like not to have any problems."

Ben, her 20-month-old toddler, was the antithesis of Ann. Whereas Ann struggled to muster the strength to parent one more day, stay sober one more day, Ben charged through life with unbridled enthusiasm for everything he saw and did and he tried to see and do everything. Ben had a body that was sturdy and compact, built for action. He moved constantly, and Ann could frequently be seen shadowing him, hunched forward with arms extended as if ready to prevent an accident, while she alternately pleaded, warned, admonished, and smacked him with her hand. Ann's awareness that she needed help in being a good parent to Ben brought her to the Parenting Program, but not until long after she began to need help in parenting her son.

When Ben was taken from Ann by Child Protective Services, she and Ben were living with her husband's mother. They had recently moved from another state, against Ann's wishes, to be close to her husband's family, and Ann was angry at Mike for uprooting her. In her words, "I'm in a place where he took me away from all my support, all my friends. And it was just him drinking, threatening me all the time, and threatening to take the baby."

Drinking and fighting were not unusual for Ann and Mike. Ann could recall only 1 year during their relationship when Mike was free of drugs and sober, and even then their relationship was volatile. Ann described the circumstances of their relationship prior to Ben's removal:

"We were separated when the situation happened. I was living with his mother. He dumped me and Ben . . . at his mom's and said if he didn't get rid of me he would probably kill me."

Ann had periodic bouts of depression during the 9 months following Ben's birth, and she recalled that her depression worsened after they moved. "If people walked up behind me," Ann said, "I just jumped, and I was shaking all the time." She found out about a women's group through a local mental health agency and attended the group for 3 weeks. Although the time she spent in therapy was not sufficient to help Ann with her depression, it was long enough for the mental health staff to question Ann's ability to parent. The following incident reinforced their concerns.

Mike's mother had assumed responsibility for most of Ben's care, but one Sunday she went to church and left Ben with Ann. Ann described what occurred after her mother-in-law left them alone.

> [Mike's mother] just took over and I couldn't do anything with him. I couldn't feed [him] — he wouldn't eat for me. He wouldn't do anything for me. So [Mike's family] just went to church that one day and left me there. I tried to feed him, and I let it go on for about a good 20 minutes before I, you know. I tried feeding him, and he was spitting [food] all over me. So then I tried the bottle, cutting off the nipple. If you've ever been hit by a plastic bottle, [you know] it hurts. [He hit me] in the face [with it] . . . we were sitting on the couch and he just threw himself back and hit me. And I just stood him up, and I just said, "Now, Ben, stop it." [Ann demonstrated how she held the baby upright and gave him an abrupt shake.] Then my mother-in-law came home, and I was sitting there crying because it was the first time I had ever been aggressive with him. And it didn't hurt him. [It made him] stop. I got his attention. He was in the crib crying [when] my mother-in-law came home, and I told her what happened.

Ann's mother-in-law called her physician who reported the incident to Child Protective Services. Ann's counselor had made a report at about the same time, after Ann had said to her, "I really need some help here because I'm afraid for me and my son." Meanwhile, Ann's mother-in-law was receiving services from a counselor at the same mental health clinic, and, according to Ann, her mother-in-law's counselor and her own counselor compared notes and exchanged confidential information about Ann's case. Ann's counselor reported her concerns about Ann's parenting to CPS without again talking to her, and the next time Ann went to mental health for counseling, Ann said, "They know what's going to happen, and they keep me over at mental health, and they just go in and take him. I never . . . because after that I had an emotional breakdown." Ann's voice became quiet as she told me, "I ended up in the psychiatric ward because I just had a breakdown."

The day that Ann was placed in the psychiatric ward of the hospital, Ben was placed in temporary foster care. About a week later, the court placed Ben with Ann's mother-in-law at the request of Ann's CPS caseworker. Ann's husband Mike was still living on his own, and according to Ann, "drinking and doing drugs." Ann expressed frustration about not being heard or believed by CPS caseworkers.

> *Ann*: Everybody's saying you're abusing your child, and I said, "No. I am not." And people were telling me what happened that day, and I'd say, "You're full of shit and you were not there. I was the only one in the house. You do not know what happened." I mean I had people telling me what I did . . . and nobody was there but me. It's just shit. It's bullshit.
>   In a . . . small town, you know — have you ever played that game where you sit in a circle and one person says something, and it goes around a circle and by the time it gets back to you it's totally not even what you said at all? That's what happened to me. But in a very serious matter.
> *Susan*: How did Ben end up at your mother-in-law's house? She got custody, right? And Mike?
> *Ann*: Right. Well, because Child Protective Services won't [place him], because it costs them money to put a child in a foster home. If the child has family, they'll place them with the family. You know what I'm saying?
> *Susan*: So let me get this straight. Your mother-in-law was the one who accused you of abusing, she filed the complaint, and she got custody of the child?
> *Ann*: Yes.
> *Susan*: And when you say you had a breakdown, tell me what you mean.
> *Ann*: Well, I was thinking about killing myself, and crying all the time, and my shaking got worse, and I couldn't sleep, and I couldn't eat.

Child Protective Services had concerns about Ann's anger, so while Ben was with his grandmother, a restraining order was issued to keep Ann from seeing her son. According to Ann, Mike was permitted unlimited visits. Ann said that while she was in the hospital, her counselor persuaded her to leave Mike. When she was released after a week, she had no job and no place to live, so she found sheltered housing. Mike was drinking everyday, according to Ann, and she, after finding a job, "didn't do anything but go to work and come home and cry and wish [she] had [her] baby."

The absence of the familial resources that are so important during the period when babies are first born to parents was common to many parents in the program — to Ann at age 29, and to Pauline who, like Jean, was still a child herself when she became a parent.

Pauline

Pauline was a 19-year-old young woman who looked her age with her clear and youthful complexion, short and shiny, wavy blonde hair, and dimples. Pauline looked like the kind of girl who would have been called a tomboy a few decades ago. She was stocky and muscular, moved purposefully, and wore flannel shirts and blue jeans that looked as if they were designed for function rather than fashion. Pauline was friendly and likable. She talked readily and clearly articulated her thoughts. She was forthright and took a no nonsense approach in her interactions with others.

Pauline's only child, Cody, had just celebrated his third birthday when the study began. Cody looked as if he had been cloned from Pauline. His rosy cheeks, dimples, and beautiful blue eyes, which tilted slightly at the corners, mirrored his mother's appearance. Cody was as serene as Ben was rambunctious, and he frequently played quietly by himself, stopping now and then to show a toy or make a comment to his mom.

Pauline's case with Child Protective Services had been closed following Cody's return to his mom from foster care a year earlier. But being a single parent was still difficult and the Parenting Program was a place Pauline knew she could go when she needed help. There weren't many places like that in Pauline's life.

Four years before I met her at the Parenting Program, Pauline, at age 15, became pregnant and went to live with her father, stepmother, and younger siblings in a city several hours north of her hometown. Her relationship with her stepmother was uncomfortable, but because her birth mother suffered from chronic mental illness, Pauline had nowhere else to live.

Pauline celebrated her 16th birthday just before giving birth to a son, Cody. Cody was born a month premature weighed 5 pounds, 13 ounces, and had a number of medical problems, including "a hole in his heart, high blood pressure, a hole in his lung, and jaundice and everything else." The baby's birth increased the tension on the already strained relationship between Pauline and her stepmother until, a month after Cody was born, Pauline's stepmother, "kicked [her] out, which," Pauline said, "was fine with me since I didn't want to live there no more anyway."

Pauline left and she and Cody went to live with Cody's father. In a short time, their relationship also became impossible, and 10 months later Pauline left Cody's father because, "He hit Cody with a leather belt. Cody was about 11 months old. Cody was just tantruming because he was cutting teeth, and he was a baby. I ain't gonna let nobody hit on my child." When Pauline left Cody's father, she handed Cody to him along with instructions to take him to his grandparents' for 2 days until she could come back for him. Pauline telephoned Cody's grandparents 2 hours after Cody and his father left in her truck, but they had not arrived. Pauline described the panic she felt not knowing where they were: "Cody was on high blood pressure medication, and without his medication, he could have some fatal problems. So I got really upset and called the police and [they] put an APB out on him. I finally did get Cody back the next day, but his [father's] whole family turned against me because of the fact that I did call the police against him."

The family retaliated, according to Pauline, by reporting her to CPS. "The way I picture it," Pauline said, "even though I don't really know how they all went about their phone calls . . . I could picture the whole group dialing CPS and everyone of them just taking their turn. And that's the way I picture it. I know it's a little different than that, but . . . he's got a big family, and his whole family got angry."

Pauline and Cody were staying temporarily at the home of some relatives of Cody's father when a CPS caseworker arrived to investigate the report. Pauline described the caseworker's instructions: "We set up a contract, and I had to follow [what it said] day-by-day. I would have to talk to him in two weeks and if things weren't going as planned, then there would be other actions taken. They said I wasn't taking Cody to the doctor and I wasn't giving him his medication, and these were the types of things that I had to do: that I had to give him breakfast, lunch, and dinner at such and such a time, make sure he gets his pills at such and such a time."

After the initial visit from her CPS caseworker, Pauline remained with her in-laws 2 weeks. The relative of Cody's father with whom Pauline and Cody resided reported Pauline to CPS a second time. Pauline maintained that the report to CPS was made without just cause.

Pauline explained, "She got mad because I told her I was going to move out . . . She didn't like the fact that I was going to do that because then she couldn't have my welfare money, then she wouldn't have a babysitter." The caseworker visited Pauline a second time. Pauline talked to the caseworker and explained "everything that was going on," but the caseworker, apparently unconvinced, handed Pauline a subpoena to appear in court the following day.

The next day when Pauline arrived at the courthouse, a court-appointed attorney approached her, introduced himself, and according to Pauline, said, "'If you'd like, you don't have to have me as your attorney. You can choose somebody else or you can hire your own.'" She answered, "'Well, I can't hire my own. You're here, I'll take you.'" Pauline described her appearance in court.

> We went in, and basically I didn't have anything to do with anything. I didn't get to speak for myself or anything. They said I had a drinking problem. They said I hit Cody with the palm of my hand. They said I couldn't [do] the things I was supposed to do like take him to the doctor, and they said I wouldn't give him the medication when I was supposed to. The judge said that since, on the petition, [it said that] my mom was mentally handicapped and emotionally unstable and my dad's whereabouts were unknown, they felt they should put me in a foster home. They said the real reason was because of the law that they could not let me out on my own unless I was 18 years old, unless I was legally emancipated.

A CPS caseworker transported Cody to a foster home, and then took Pauline to lunch before transporting her to the same foster home. "This was the first part that was really bad," Pauline told me. "Two children in the foster home had hepatitis. I lived in fear for 2 days. Cody was at the crawling stage and the toddler who was ill was trying to bite and scratch and pinch Cody." Pauline asked for permission to visit a friend and when she and Cody arrived at her friend's house, she called CPS and "told them plain flat out, either I would be staying here, or you put me in another foster home. Don't make no difference to me. I want to go by the rules. I don't want to go against you people. I want to work and get back on my own."

CPS did not acquiesce to Pauline's demands. A caseworker took Pauline and Cody back to the foster home, and made plans to move them a short time later only because their foster parent was having surgery. The only foster care home CPS could find that could take both Pauline and Cody was in a distant town that seemed very far away to Pauline. She described her reaction to the move.

> I had no idea where it was. I knew it was near the coast and that was it. I was not going someplace where I didn't know where I was going. So I took Cody, June 5th, about 4:00 — or about 1:00 o'clock in the morning, and I took [him], and I ran, and I was gone for about 3½ weeks. They found me, and they picked me up. From there . . . we went from the place I was at to the police station. That was the last time [I saw] Cody. When we got to the police station they took me in to arrest me, because . . . they were pressing kidnapping charges on [me for taking] my own child because he was a ward of the court. You know, I had no understanding that they were going to arrest me for kidnapping my own child. I was upset. And they took Cody's medication, Cody's clothes, and they took him. And he was gone. I never even got to say good-bye, give him a hug, or nothing.

FAMILY HISTORIES

When children are maltreated, it is usually in their homes by family members (American Humane Association, 1986). Although assault by day-care providers or strangers captures media and public attention, it is relatively atypical. Nearly 90% of all incidents of maltreatment occur in children's homes by a parent or other relative (Bronfenbrenner, 1974, cited in Garbarino, 1976; American Humane Association, 1986). Data from the American Humane Association (1986) indicate that incidents of maltreatment by people who are unrelated to the child occur in only 11.9% of reported cases nationwide. What happens to children when those people who are ultimately responsible for their health, development, well-being — indeed, their lives — provide environments that are inconsistent, psychologically, socially and physically impoverished, or dangerous?

This very important question is not directly addressed in this study, nor is the impact of maltreatment on children readily apparent from the transcripts of interviews or observations and descriptions that appear here. Children were mentioned by parents and Parenting Program staff less often than I anticipated when I began conducting the study. As I reviewed my field notes and transcripts, the absence of children seemed conspicuous. This study is, nevertheless, pertinent to maltreated children, regardless of the infrequency with which they were mentioned. But it is not only about the children of parents in the program and study, whose psychological, social, emotional, cognitive, language, and physical development may be affected by abuse and neglect in real and lasting ways, it is also about yesterday's children, the parents themselves. As is evident from the parents' stories of the circumstances surrounding their involvement with CPS, during childhood and continuing into their adult years they were essentially without the support and emotional bonds inherent in Frost's description of home as "the place where, when you have to go there / They have to take you in."

Jean

Jean's life, like that of many parents in the program, was in continuous flux. But, unlike those parents who had no family available, Jean's days were inundated with relatives — sometimes welcome, sometimes not. As we spoke at different times, and sometimes on the same day, Jean's descriptions of and feelings about her family seemed to rapidly change. When I inquired about her family, she spoke of her children before mentioning her parents and siblings. Her stories, whether she talked about her parents or her children, revealed relationships that were tortuous and roles that were tangled and confused. At age 6 her maternal uncle began sexually abusing her, she became a parent while still a child at the age of 14, and her brother sexually abused her eldest two daughters when they were not yet school age. According to some staff at the program, her 6- and 7-year-old daughters were more like parents than children to Jean.

When talking about her family of origin, Jean expressed great love for her father, who had died several years earlier after battling chronic emphysema and asthma. She blamed her mother for his death, explaining that her mother had pushed his wheelchair by an open door when it was "freezing, and she turned up the heat full blast." Her father "caught pneumonia and died," according to Jean, "because he had the hot air hitting him, and the cold air hitting him." Jean said that when the paramedics arrived her father couldn't breathe and was covered with frost. Jean said that she talked to her mom "maybe three times" during the 4 years since her father's death. "I hate her," she explained, "she hates me, and we have a mutual agreement."

Jean's feelings about her mother were rooted in a time prior to her father's death when her mother behaved as if "she didn't care about anyone." Jean described her mother's behavior:

My dad always saved money for us kids and my mom never did . . . She went grocery shopping and she'd buy a little bit of food, and the rest she'd spend on [herself]. My dad would have to go out and take his money out and do the grocery shopping because she spent all the food stamps on pop and candy and stuff.

Jean saw herself as a scapegoat, and described her mother as good to her siblings but not to her. Her dad, she said, "was terrific. He handled things right. He never spanked us."

Jean's problems with family were not only with her mother. The "rape" she experienced by her uncle continued from when she was 6 until she was 12. Within 2 years after the sexual abuse stopped, Jean, at the age of 14, became a parent. Jean did not disclose the abuse to anyone until she left home. During an argument with her mother, she divulged that her uncle had sexually abused her, but her mother expressed disbelief. The maltreatment remained unacknowledged in Jean's family and unresolved in her own mind. Jean wondered if she was somehow responsible: "I really felt like there was something I could have done or should have done. But at the time, I felt like I did the right thing. And I'm sure I probably did."

Ann

Susan: If you could paint a picture of your family, what would it look like?

Ann: That's pretty easy. It is jet black, cloudy. I'm trying not to cry. I would draw a heart that's broken. And I would draw kids that are crying.

Susan: Who would the kids be?

Ann: Me, my brother. Cloudy, black. Broken heart. And the kids crying.

Ann described her childhood as "average." She was adopted during infancy by a family that also adopted a second child. She remembered living in an "ordinary" home as a toddler, then moving to a home on a golf course as her father's business grew more successful. Her parents traveled frequently, leaving Ann and her brother at home with live-in caregivers. She thought her family's changing economic situation roughly coincided with the onset of violence in the family, but she did not recall exactly how it started.

Incidents of physical abuse started when she was about 12. When Ann and her brother argued, her mother, Ann said, "couldn't control us, and that would make my dad mad. Then they'd start fighting, and he'd start hitting her." Ann stood between her parents and told her father, "Hit me, hit me," and he would. Ann described her father's behavior:

He'd just go into these rages. Like, if he came home and me and my mom were arguing or something like that, he'd get really mad and start hitting. He hit with his fist sometimes. He used to wear those big skull men's rings, you know those colored rings with [a] stone — and the stone would leave these little bruise marks on my arms. He used to take a belt to me most of the time. He'd start hitting me, and he couldn't stop. Just like with my mom, he'd start hitting her, and it took me screaming at him most of the time to stop . . . I remember all sorts of incidents, like sitting at the dinner table and having a beer glass go flying across the table, with forks and knives flying across the table.

Ann attributed the violence in part to her mother who "had a mouth on her . . . and just never knew when to quit." She described her mother as "caustic." Ann remembered spending time in her room feeling upset and angry, but believing she had no one to ask for help. "I couldn't ever do anything," she explained, "because if I tried to tell her how I felt, she'd say, 'Don't talk back,' or, 'Don't be belligerent.' So I did a lot of acting out, a lot of acting out, because I couldn't get any good attention any other way, and I couldn't express how I was feeling." Ann provided examples of what she meant by "acting out":

I punched walls and put my hands through windows and punched people. And then I turned to drugs, I turned it in on myself, and I was very self-destructive. Because I think when you resort to putting a needle in your arm, that's the ultimate destructive behavior towards yourself.

Ann began using drugs and alcohol at age 13, and, in her words, has "done everything." During the following 3 years Ann began having trouble at school, ran away from home, and, with an acquaintance who was prostituting, had her first sexual experience with a stranger on the street from whom she contracted gonorrhea. At 16 she was placed by her parents in an institution for girls with problem behavior. Ann said that she remained in the institution for 1½ years, and while there put razor blades in her mouth, ate cleanser, put her foot through a wire window, broke windows with her fists, and yanked hair from the staff members' heads when they tried to restrain her.

Released from the institution when she was 18, no longer welcome in her parents' home, and having recently inherited $10,000 from her grandmother's estate, Ann was on her own. She spent the entire sum of money in 8 months buying heroin and crystal methamphetamine. She became pregnant by a man she described as a heroin junkie, and had an abortion at her parents' insistence. At 19, out of money and resources, Ann moved in with a man 50 years her senior who gave her food, shelter, and drugs in exchange for sex.

Ann's life was a series of drugs, social programs, and brief relationships with men until in her early twenties she married her first husband, and at twenty-three gave birth to a daughter. Ann and her husband used drugs and alcohol, and Ann was accused of neglecting her infant daughter by CPS. When the child was 10 months of age, she was removed from her home by CPS.

Ann maintained contact with her daughter until the child was 2, at which time she allowed her daughter to be adopted—a decision she described as "the right thing." When I asked if she felt comfortable with her decision, she answered, "Yes. Why shouldn't I? I loved that child enough to let her go to a home where there's no drinking, no smoking, no drugs . . . So why should I feel bad? And even though people try to use that against me, I will not feel bad about it. Because there's one kid out of how many kids that got saved and got put in a good, sound home." She paused and lowered her voice, "Of course, when they first took her from me I had a hard time with it. I tried to commit suicide three times."

Pauline

> To paint a picture of my family would be to draw me and my mom and my sister on one side [of] a dam like you see at the river, and then [on the other side] you'd find my dad, my stepmom, my other sisters, and my brother. And the reason why it's like that is because my dad basically has taken that part of the family away from us.

Pauline, her mother, and sister had "limited communication" with her father and siblings during the 9 years following her parents' divorce and child custody battle. About the time of the divorce, when Pauline was 10 years of age, her mother had a "nervous breakdown." Her father took her mother to court and "used her illness against her to get custody" of Pauline and her sisters. Pauline's father testified that his wife "was crazy and couldn't take care of her children," and he accused her of physically abusing Pauline's 18-month-old sister.

Pauline testified in court on her father's behalf. She was influenced, she said, by her father telling her "over and over and over and over that my mother never loved me." Despite having been physically and sexually abused by her father, Pauline listened to and chose to live with him. When she appeared in court, Pauline told the judge, "I don't want to live with my mom. My mom don't love me."

During the 6 years following her parents' divorce, from the age of 10 until she turned 16 and became pregnant with Cody, Pauline had limited contact with her mother. She lived with her stepmother, siblings, and father, who "hopped from state to state" to keep ahead of creditors trying to collect back payments for rent-to-own merchandise he "bought" and took with him each time the family moved. After Cody was born and Pauline's stepmother told her to leave, 16-year-old Pauline seemed to have more liabilities than resources: a baby with heart and lung disease, a mother with a history of mental illness, a boyfriend who was abusive, and problems with her own use of alcohol. Her situation deteriorated to the point where it became obvious to those around her that something must be done. The something was a report to CPS by Pauline's in-laws who complained of her negligent parenting, and the result was legal intervention through CPS and the court system.

The stories in this chapter illustrate the kinds of desperate situations that families are experiencing when they are reported by concerned, or angry, or perhaps frustrated professionals, family, or neighbors — situations that are so much less clear than the stereotypic notions society holds about abusive parents and abused children. These are the confused, uncertain, ambiguous circumstances those at CPS must swiftly sort out in order to make a determination of the validity of the complaint and the course of action they should take to protect the children involved. These are the reports that precipitate a series of events that can inalterably change the lives of children and families in ways that may or may not eventually benefit them.

CHAPTER 3

CHILD PROTECTIVE SERVICES—
PREVENTION AND INTERVENTION

The most common offenses alleged of parents in the Parenting Program were physical maltreatment, which occurred in 20 families, and neglect, which occurred in 23 families. More than one-fourth of the parents enrolled in the program had been indicted by Child Protective Services (CPS) because they had failed to protect their children from physical maltreatment by another person, and 7 parents had failed to protect their children from sexual maltreatment. Another 7 parents had given birth to infants whom they had exposed to drugs or alcohol during pregnancy. Two parents had abandoned their children. Fifteen of the 55 parents enrolled in the program were alleged by Child Protective Services to have committed multiple offenses of child maltreatment.

Few parents in the Parenting Program admitted to seeing themselves as abusive. They offered examples of abuse—bruises, broken bones, cigarette burns—as evidence that they knew what abuse was and it wasn't what had "happened to them." Families that participated in the Parenting Program were involved with CPS for a number of different reasons. Not all of the incidents that marked their entry into the child welfare system were as obvious as burns or broken bones. The assignment of blame or responsibility for alleged incidents of maltreatment among families in the Parenting Program is clouded by the contexts in which the maltreatment had occurred and the complexity of the families' lives that is so evident in the parents' stories of their initial involvement with the CPS system. How is child abuse identified and substantiated in situations riddled with untruths and confusion by a system that operates with "no useful legal or scientific definition of abuse and neglect" (Gelles, 1979, p. 24)?

SUBSTANTIATING CHILD MALTREATMENT

The process of verifying abuse from circumstantial evidence—a process described by Elmer (1977) as "dubious at best"—was an issue with parents. Documentation gathered for my study and this book from

CPS case files, interviews with caseworkers, and a survey designed to track characteristics of children and families in the program, their use of services, and outcomes of intervention, provide descriptions of the families and situations that brought them to CPS and the Parenting Program. From the perspectives of parents, however, that documentation does not accurately portray the entire story. An excerpt from an interview with Ann illustrates the complexity of many situations in which abuse or neglect is suspected by CPS.

> *Susan*: When I hear you talk about all the painful stuff that was going on when CPS got involved, it makes me think you really did need some kind of help at the time.
>
> *Ann*: I was asking for help. I was asking for help, but I didn't know where to go. I had only been in town for a month. But I don't think it was the right kind of help—to take my child. Because that just made matters worse. I was on the verge of having an emotional breakdown when it happened, and when it happened, I had it for sure. Then while I was in treatment, I couldn't get anywhere, and I couldn't accomplish anything because I was so upset and I had all these upsetting phone calls. They just took the baby . . . So, I didn't get any help. Yeah, I needed help and I could have got the help I needed, I think, and still kept my child. . . . That part I disagree with because I was asking for help, because I knew what was going on was wrong. . . . They think that's the way they helped me, [by taking] my child.
>
> But to a degree, I agree because the situation was not good for him. But then to another degree, I mean, I self reported. It wasn't like I was beating up on my kid and got reported from 15 different people. Okay, so it was kind of "iffy." Then I got blamed for the whole thing. And I'm a danger to my son, and I don't belong with my son, and all of a sudden if Mike is going to divorce me and file for full custody, then [CPS] will drop the case. . . . That I did not agree with, and I felt really railroaded. . . .
>
> *Susan*: Paint a different scenario. What would have been helpful to you at that time? What would have been a better way, not only for you, but for Ben and the whole family?
>
> *Ann*: Well, I think personally that Ben should have gone into a foster home, been kept totally out of the picture, because there was too much, with him being with his grandmother and then Mike having unlimited visitations and me having none, there was too much using Ben as a pawn. [Imitating Mike:] "If you don't do

this, you won't see Ben again, and if you report me for breaking your finger, you won't see Ben again." So I think he should have gone to a foster home, and then instead of [CPS] totally focusing in on me, I think since we were a family, the whole family should have been investigated as a family instead of singling me out and letting Mike have unlimited visitations. All he did was get drunk and cause more problems that way. So I think . . . [that] since we were a family, it should have been dealt with as a family.

Isabelle, who co-directed the Parenting Program with Georgia, talked about the problem of substantiating suspected incidents of abuse among parents enrolled in the program: "I think that in the context of our program, we often, as a group, decide whether we should report specific incidents that happen and I don't always know whether I should, but usually I report if I'm in doubt and let the agency decide. We go by the policy that we aren't the investigators, and that we have to think of the child first and foremost. If there's a question of the child being abused in any way, we will report to CPS."

Meeting legal requirements is one reason that professionals report incidents of child abuse and situations believed to be harmful to children to CPS. However, reports of suspected child maltreatment by professionals who work with children and families are motivated, in my opinion, by the desire to do something to help children they believe to be in truly desperate situations. Intervention does occur subsequent to reports and substantiation of maltreatment, but it is questionable whether it ever benefits children or addresses the concerns of those who issued reports.

LEGAL INTERVENTION

When a report is made to CPS, whether by the Parenting Program or another source, the policy of CPS is to send a caseworker to interview the children or the parents or both depending upon the severity of the situation and ages of the children. If the caseworker believes the children are in imminent danger or are afraid to return to their parents, they are removed from their home by a caseworker who is accompanied by a police officer. Once children are removed from their home, they are placed in a temporary shelter home for a period of not longer than 30 days, then they are transferred to a foster home. Although 30 days is the legal limit for temporary placement, Georgia reported that place-

ments might last longer because of chronic shortages of approved foster care homes and the limited number of multiple slots available in a single home that would allow siblings to be placed together. Locating placements for children with emotional and behavioral disorders, medical problems, developmental delays, or disabilities puts additional demands on an already overtaxed system.

Within 24 hours following the removal of children from their home, a court hearing is held. CPS presents information about the circumstances of the children's removal to the court and based on that information, a judge determines whether the children should be returned to their parents or whether the state should retain custody. If the court rules that the state should retain custody, the judge schedules a fact finding that occurs within 30 days and is likened by Georgia to a trial in which CPS proves they are "right and the parents did these bad things, or the parent proves they didn't do these bad things. Or the parent can stipulate right there, and say, 'Yes, I did this.'" According to Georgia, fact findings have taken as long as 6 months. During that time, children in foster homes remain there, often for protracted periods of time. The median time children spent in foster care in the county in which the Parenting Program was based was 22 months.[2] (The mean length of time or the range of time children spent in foster care placements was not reported by CPS.) On average, children lived in 2 separate foster care placements during each year they were in the custody of the state. Reports to CPS marked the beginning of legal proceedings that could take families years to resolve.

Frequently aired complaints from parents in the Parenting Program reflected their frustration over the lack of opportunities to tell their stories and over not being believed when they did offer information. They expressed shock and anger about the removal of their children, outrage that someone would have the power to take something that was theirs. Pauline emphasized the words "my own child" during an interview, and Jean stressed that "those are my kids." When I asked Ann what she thought the expectations of CPS were, what they wanted, she answered, "My son."

Ann's description of her experience in the court system after Ben's removal from home leaves the impression that the legal system has as little credibility with her as does CPS.

---

[2]Data describing the length of foster care placements were obtained from the Child Protective Services Agency in the county in which this study was conducted. A citation is omitted in order to protect the privacy of the people, programs, and locations in this study.

Ann: It's like a year down the line and they didn't even put me in front of the judge and charge me with child abuse.

Susan: They never formally charged you?

Ann: No. But they sure made it sound like I was some big danger to my son and that I literally shook him so hard that . . . [it all] got so blown out of proportion and sounded so terrible. No, they never brought me up on charges. And . . . [the caseworker] finally admitted that she knew I never abused him.

Susan: Did she say why [CPS] was involved?

Ann: Because he was *at risk*. He was *at risk*. [Ann emphasized her words.]

Susan: What does that mean?

Ann: That there are possibilities that he might be abused.

Susan: I wonder what their expectations were. What do you think they wanted out of all this?

Ann: My son.

Susan: How did you figure out what was going on?

Ann: I never really did. I mean, God, I went up in front of the judge maybe twice, and he's looking through his papers, and he's going, "I don't know what the hell's going on here." And no papers were ever signed, and he was constantly saying he never knew what was going on. And he's gone on vacation and [another judge] would make a decision, then he'd come back and reverse the decision. He never even knew what was going on half the time.

Susan: This all occurred in [the other city]?

Ann: Yeah.

Susan: So when you said no papers were signed, you mean. . . .

Ann: Well, he was going through the papers. I don't know what kind of papers. And he was getting upset because he didn't know what was going on, and he had a bunch of papers in front of him that never got signed, and they were lost in a stack of his papers. He said one time, he went on vacation, then he came back and he ordered that Mike could have custody or something, I don't remember, and then he comes back and said, "If I would have known what I was signing, I never would have signed it."

Susan: The judge said this?

Ann: Yeah. He didn't even know what was going on half the time.

Susan: What was he referring to when he said, "If I had known what I was signing, I never would have signed it"?

Ann: I think it was papers giving Mike full custody the first time. Then I stood up and said, "I want my child — if I can't have him, then I want him put in foster care." He signed some kind of orders, I can't remember, I think it was giving him custody the first time. And he said, "Oh is this the [Ben's surname] case? If I had known that, I never would have signed the papers." The judge didn't even know half the time what was going on. I never even got to tell the judge my side of the story.

Parents expressed feelings of helplessness about their situations — in Ann's words, being "railroaded" by the system. Pauline was dismayed that she had to appear in court the day after she was served a subpoena. Although mandating court appearances within 24 hours after the removal of children from their homes was designed to protect the rights of parents as well as children, an appearance in court seemed to add confusion and intimidation to situations that were already complex and emotionally charged. The trauma felt by parents as a result of abrupt separation from their children seemed to be exacerbated by miscommunication between parents and caseworkers. For some parents it marked the beginning of an adversarial relationship with a system whose mission it was to protect children from parents who were, I suspect, the people the children loved and wanted most to be with.

Of the three parents in this study, Jean's description of what occurred before she went to court was the exception to the norm, and perhaps provides a clue as to what should but frequently does not happen: "It was all very new to me. Very new . . . after they explained to me what was going on, and the circumstances and stuff, and the depth of all this, I said, 'okay.' I walked out of there and I felt really secure about where they were at. My caseworker explained everything in detail to me. She even explained the court proceedings, and we sat there for a good 2 hours talking."

The events that precipitated allegations of child maltreatment by CPS were different for each of the three families. Although Jean's children were clearly harmed, and one might argue that Ann's and Pauline's children also were harmed, intentional harm on the part of the three parents was less certain. Family situations were extremely complex when CPS staff investigated and abuse and neglect were difficult to identify and define. These situations made it all the more remarkable that CPS staff focused their intervention on one person rather than on parents and children in the contexts of their families.

When families cannot or will not perform the roles and functions our society expects of parents, such as providing physical and emotional warmth, nurturance, food, medical care, and guidance for their children, society may intervene forcefully, as with the legal intervention that frequently results after child maltreatment is substantiated. In the Parenting Program, however, an alternative approach to addressing child maltreatment is used.

THE PARENTING PROGRAM

Abuse and neglect of children has come to be regarded by our society as a problem that is very prevalent and very serious, but also preventable. Although there is not a great body of empirical evidence about prevention of maltreatment, during the last 20 years the number of primary, secondary, and tertiary treatment approaches has increased along with an awareness of the phenomena we refer to as child abuse (Olds & Henderson, 1989). The Parenting Program is an example of a tertiary treatment program, one designed to treat children who have already experienced abuse and to prevent future occurrences of abuse. The Parenting Program, like many across the nation, started as a small project by a volunteer women's organization. The program provided respite care to parents who had abused or neglected their children while their children attended daycare. As time passed and child maltreatment received increased recognition by society as a significant problem, the program grew — it served more children and began to offer services that were increasingly specialized and comprehensive.

An Ecological Approach to the Prevention of Child Maltreatment

Many intervention approaches for child maltreatment have been developed recently (instruction in parenting theory and skills, anger management, individual and group counseling, parent support groups, enhancement of parent-child [typically mother-child] interactions, telephone hotlines, crisis care, respite care, home-health visits [Olds & Henderson, 1989]), but what sets the Parenting Program apart is its behavioral and ecological approaches to intervention.

Within an ecological framework, human development is understood in terms of the progressive, mutual accommodations people and their environments make over the life span. Relations between people within their immediate settings, as well as the larger formal and informal social contexts in which people and settings are embedded, are the basis of an ecological framework (Bronfenbrenner, 1977). Bronfenbrenner's conceptual model includes four levels, each level nested within a level broader in scope than the previous one. The first level, the microsystem, consists of relationships between the developing person and the immediate environment, such as the child within foster care, intervention, and home care settings. The second level, the mesosystem, refers to the interrelations among the multiple settings in which the person develops. The mesosystem, in relation to the families in the Parenting Program, might lead one to examine the congruence between the resources available in home settings and the demands of intervention and CPS settings, and their mutual influence on the outcomes of intervention. The third level, the exosystem, extends the concept of the mesosystem to include other formal and informal social structures that influence the developing person, such as the ways interventions are conceptualized by CPS caseworkers, and the process by which children and families enter and exit the system. The fourth and broadest level of the ecological model, the macrosystem, refers to cultural values, attitudes, and patterns of our economic, social, education, legal and political systems that are manifest in the three previous levels. At this level, consider the outcome that occurs in a society that does not assure health care for all citizens. A family in that society that cannot afford medical services has a child who acquires a hearing impairment from untreated chronic ear infections, and the child's inability to hear is misinterpreted by teachers and family as an unwillingness to comply with directions. The impact of policies at the broadest level are visited on the parent-child, teacher-child, and teacher-parent relationships.

Intervention based on an ecological framework combines a number of different treatment strategies in an attempt to address the problem of maltreatment from different levels of intervention. It considers the relationship between the developing child and parent not only in intervention settings but also in home and foster home settings, within the context of family and other social networks, and within the larger contexts of neighborhoods and communities. The ecological framework includes a recognition of the mutual influence of the developing person and the organizational and cultural environments in which the person exists. An ecological intervention approach to prevent child maltreatment represents an important shift from traditional interventions that focus exclusively on treating the maltreated child or the adult accused of having maltreated the child to interventions that address the problem in the contexts of families and communities in which such maltreatment occurs.

The Parenting Program attempts to focus intervention on all members of an immediate family rather than solely on the maltreated child.

The program takes into account the dynamics of parent-child characteristics and relationships by providing assessments of children's developmental status and level of functioning, and assessment and intervention for parent-child interactions in typical contexts. The program began moving intervention out of clinical settings into the homes and communities of families and providing intervention during home visits and in laundromats, in grocery stores, and on city buses.

When families initially enter the Parenting Program (most of them mandated to attend), they receive 16 hours of didactic training in 5 different areas: child development, behavior management, child safety, nutrition, and problem solving. One staff person (or family interventionist as they were called) is assigned to one or two families so that families and staff might develop close working relationships. The services offered by the program are based on the belief that intervention should be comprehensive in content and include instruction in clearly identified and defined skills that are mutually agreed upon by parents, staff, and caseworkers; should teach skills in ways that promote generalized use in settings outside of the intervention classroom; should be individualized and flexible based on each family's unique history, individual strengths, and particular needs; should consider the relationship between parent and child as transactional (Sameroff & Chandler, 1975) and existing within the contexts of extended family and community; and should be facilitative and supportive in order to enable and empower families (Dunst, Trivette, & Deal, 1988; Patterson & Chamberlain, 1990).

The program is designed to provide behavioral intervention within an experiential framework, as well as didactic training. The behavioral approach, based on the teachings of the work of Skinner (1953), Bijou (1966), and others, emphasizes that behavior occurs as a function of the environment. Within a behavioral model of intervention, the responsibility (and blame) for failure to acquire a given skill shifts from the learner, the "bad parent," to the teacher, the Parenting Program interventionist. Georgia, the program co-director and one of the founders of the Parenting Program, described during an audiotaped interview how the program came about and how it functions.

> I started working for CPS 6 years ago doing parent training. They had me teaching classes at night — behavior management and child development, anger management and communication . . . and I would have parents who would do very well. For example, I would do unit reviews and ask them questions, "If you were in this situation and your child did this, what would your response be?" They

would all pretty much, at the end of the program, have the right answers—have really good, thoughtful, perceptive answers. So, I felt really good about that. Then I'd do these write-ups for the caseworker and let them know how parents were able to take the information and demonstrate an understanding of the information, but when I would see them in the homes with their children, or I would hear about the way they would actually behave with their children, it was quite different.

So it seemed to me that it didn't make much sense to teach them theories and ideas without giving them opportunities to practice. Many parents had children in foster care. They were seeing their children once a week in a small room at CPS for an hour. They were getting parent training classes that were simply theoretical, then visiting their child [for an] hour a week in a room that was probably about 6′ × 8′, I guess. Then, the children would be returned to them, occasionally with really dismal results, because the parents weren't prepared to have their kids back after the kids had been in foster care for a long time.

I wanted to have a parent training program that more realistically dealt with the problems the parents were having and used a minimal amount of theoretical material but enough so that we'd have a common language—[so] that if I said "reinforcing" they'd know what I was talking about, [and] if I said "cognitive," they'd know what I was talking about. We would have a common set of [terms], and they would be familiar with the ideas that I was talking about when we were with the kids. But the weight wasn't going to be on theory. The weight would be on actually having some experiences with their kids.

And we would use a behavioral approach—not only teach a behavioral approach to the parents on how to work with their kids, but we would use a behavioral approach with the parents. In other words, we would reinforce the positive behaviors that we saw in the parents and shape the sorts of behaviors that were [most] appropriate for them as parents.

Georgia described a typical day in the lab school at the Parenting Program:

The kids are in the lab with their parents, and the parent achieves a goal. Maybe one of the goals is giving directions. When they give directions, they must use clear language, get down at the child's level, state directions positively in a firm but gentle voice. And maybe it's always been an issue with that family that the child would never comply. So the parents have been pleading and begging for the child to put his plate away after lunch, and the child says, "No," and throws the plate on the floor. Then one day [one of] the parents goes up to the child, gets on the child's level, and says, "You need to put your plate away after you finish, then we can go out and play. After you put the plate away, you can go outside and play." At that moment I might look at them and smile and wink or something. Later on, I might say, "Boy, you really did it that time, and I can tell you meant it." And hopefully the child would also reinforce them by complying, or maybe comply more readily than he would have previously. That's the best reinforcer of all, when the parents try things that work. And that's why it's really good, when parents . . . come to group and say, "Gee, I tried this last week and this is what happened, and you were right, this worked." That's probably the most reinforcing. That's what I mean. Instead of focusing a lot on the things the parents are doing that aren't really working for them, we focus more on the positive things and [on] redirecting the parents toward more successful child management techniques.

The Parenting Program offers an alternative to classroom learning to parents who may have had histories of failure in classroom settings and who may have had difficulty translating the theories they heard about in class into practice with their own children. As part of the therapeutic nursery program, the Parenting Program is strengthened by strong connections with the community. It is housed in a community church that provides a more inviting place for children and parents to see each other each week than the small visitation rooms at the county CPS office. A small army of over 50 volunteers and graduate students from the university assist in all aspects of the program from administration and program evaluation to teaching, child care, and transporting children. The program is able to provide fairly comprehensive services to families in need thanks to a broad funding base that includes donations of clothing, food, and equipment from individuals and local businesses; city, county, and state funding for child abuse prevention and treatment; and federal monies for the development of exemplary model programs. Like the therapeutic nursery program of which it was a part, the Parenting Program was designed to serve families living in poverty.

The Parenting Program is where parents who are poor are required to come by the court system when their children are removed from home because of abuse and neglect, and when the local CPS agency does not believe the parents can or will provide a safe home for their children. Parents who come to the Parenting Program have few options for obtaining assistance to address the challenges of parenting because they lack the awareness and communication and advocacy skills needed to access supportive services such as educational intervention for their children, counseling, or family support; however, they are parents who are readily identified as needing emergency intervention from CPS. This was the place where parents who are seen as the most difficult to change are sent by CPS or juvenile court, often as a last resort.

Intervention in the Parenting Program

The community church in which the Parenting Program is held is familiar to many of the parents enrolled in the program. In addition to donating classroom space, kitchen facilities, toys, and equipment to the program, the church provides meeting space for Alcoholics and Narcotics Anonymous meetings. A number of parents in the program have attended those meetings at one time or another. Two blocks away, a food bank distributes grocery staples for those who run out of food or food stamps before the next month's allotment arrives.

During my observations of the Parenting Program, I saw friendly workers in the church office remain unflappable when people without homes, apparently without sanity, dressed in everything they owned, stopped by to ask for food or money. Church staff members kindly gave information or directions as if they were speaking to one of the doctors or professors from the nearby university who comprised much of the church's membership. For awhile, a homeless man who muttered incessantly to some unseen conversational partner made the garden courtyard just outside the church parlor his home. When I had to pass him I would hold my breath and hope that he would not notice me or turn his conversation to me, or I would pretend to be deep in thought so that if he spoke I would, understandably, not hear him. However, the workers in the church treated him with the same respect they accorded me and the Parent Program staff.

The church is located in a city of about 100,000 people that rests in a valley next to a blue collar mill town of about 60,000 people. The economy in the larger university town was fairly healthy during 1989 when I began the study—at least compared to the recession that ushered in the eighties and reappeared in the nineties. For parents in the program, however, life was difficult regardless of whether the majority of the population was employed. Mill jobs were not as available as they once were, and service jobs that paid minimum wage, when they could be found, were not worth pursuing because they barely paid for transportation to the job and child care.

The church is located in a neighborhood a few blocks from the university campus, where streets are lined with mature trees and small, wooden houses built during the 1920s and 1930s. A quality remains from the 1960s when people had settled in communes along the river. Politics are liberal and lifestyles are a matter of individual choice. Most staff members at the Parenting Program wear jeans or vintage clothes and jewelry from secondhand stores. They look similar to the parents who attend the program. Staff take pride in having jobs that are socially relevant and personally rewarding. If attendance, laughter, long hours, and continued commitment are an indication, they like working at the program.

Parents seem to be in friendly territory when they arrive at the program on a city bus or limp into the church parking lot in large, noisy, old American cars. There is usually someone they know smoking and leaning against the large, green trash dumpster in the alley behind the church (the place designated as the smoking area by the church in an effort to contain the cigarette butts that parents leave behind and to prevent intimidation of elderly ladies who attend the church). If a friend does not greet parents first, a staff member will say hello and call them by name, and perhaps stop to ask how they are.

As I observed one warm spring morning, parents entered the two-story brick building through the alley behind the church while the staff busily prepared the children's classrooms by arranging books, blocks, paints, and games. The sounds of a humming vacuum, a ringing phone, and the chirping of Mr. Rays, the resident canary, singing in his cage competed with Beethoven's *Ode to Joy*, which played softly on a portable audiotape player. The program's cook prepared lunch for over 50 people with the assistance of any staff person who had time to help. The menus had been designed by the parents when they were learning about nutrition in the didactic part of the program. Fresh vegetables were chopped and yogurt dip stirred, white cheese was grated (it was lower in fat and healthier than yellow cheese), and tuna was spread on whole wheat bread and bagels (donated by a local baker), then toasted in large commercial ovens. One lunchtime, while I watched children eat raw broccoli and cauliflower that was served with unflavored yogurt for dipping, a staff member explained that this kind of food may be rejected by most children, but it was readily eaten by children who were hungry.

Several staff, wearing name tags, waited in each of three classrooms while others waited outside in the alley to greet children who arrived from foster care in the CPS van or were delivered by foster parents. Staff seemed relaxed and the routine well-rehearsed, despite a warning from Georgia, one of the co-directors of the Parenting Program, to be wary of one couple that CPS caseworkers thought might attempt to flee with their three children when the children arrived at the program from foster care.

As families waited outside the church for their children to arrive, a fight erupted between Jean and her sister. Someone in the program called the police while the women struggled in the alley. Jean later told me that her sister came to the program to accuse Jean of telling her husband that she was having an affair. Jean admitted that she told her brother-in-law that her sister was "cheating on him," and explained that she said it to get back at her sister for stealing $350 from her.

After the session ended that day, Jean had X-rays taken of her neck and filed charges against her sister, but she finished the fight in time to greet two of her five children as they arrived from foster care in the van. Her two middle children, a 5-year-old daughter and a 4-year-old son, smiled as Jean reached out to help them down from the van. Her daughter greeted Jean by saying, "Mom, I have something for you." "You do-do?" Jean asked with enthusiasm and wide eyes. Jean had brought something for her children as well. To the dismay of the staff person who worked with Jean and constantly encouraged her to provide nutritious meals for her children, Jean gave them their usual treat of candy bars and a huge paper cup of Pepsi from a quick-stop market.

Parents and foster parents arrived at different entrances of the church so they would not meet face-to-face. Staff took children from the arms of the temporary parents who would spend 165 hours of each week with those children and shuttled them to the arms of their mothers and fathers who would spend the next 3 hours with them. Some parents and children greeted with kisses and embraces, some with vigilance and distance.

Once in the classroom, their activities seemed remarkable in that they were so ordinary. Were these the parents who had assaulted their children, spent grocery money for drugs, or brawled in alleys with relatives? Children and parents, mostly moms and an occasional dad, sat side by side in child-size chairs and sculpted clay or rolled paint on paper using homemade rollers of empty spools and wire. One parent stooped by her son's side to paint at his easel and to ask him about his painting. Another squeezed into a small wooden bus for a ride with her son. Children moved from one activity to another when their interest waned or when their parent's interest waned. Some parents seemed as engaged in play as their children, and one adolescent mother wrote that the activities were "awesome" on a form asking her to evaluate the program.

After a time, one of the staff asked a child to ring a bell to signal that it was time to clean up and prepare for lunch. The parents, who seemed familiar with the routine, took their children to wash their hands after the toys and materials were put away and the room was in order. Just before lunch, families gathered in a large circle on the floor and sang songs together. All the adults and most of the children participated, although one child declined with an embarrassed smile, and several others dove for their mother's arms. Children suggested personal favorites, and a staff person led them in old familiar songs. Parents and children faced each other with smiles and with hands intertwined while singing "Row Your Boat." The staff person who lead the song prompted them by saying "put your life vests on," and "go over the rocks," and Jean and her children bumped up and down together over the pretend rapids. The Parenting Program staff calmed the children before lunch by talking softly about floating on "a smooth shiny surface, sun shining on your faces, that good feeling, mosquitoes buzzing." After they sang "Twinkle Twinkle Little Star," a child was chosen to touch each person in turn with a magic wand and dismiss them for lunch. Then families gathered together at one of the three small preschool tables and chairs.

Lunch was served family style in pretty, old china and with mixed patterned silver cutlery borrowed from the church. Families and staff were interspersed at the low tables. In one room, the whole group joined hands before eating and said, "For family, friends, and food, we thank you." In all three rooms I heard quiet conversations throughout lunch — mostly between adults — about how to cook certain dishes and which foods their children liked best.

Some children were quiet, while others talked during the meal. Staff would comment about a particular child's activities and prompt conversations with parents in an effort to encourage the children's language development and promote the parents' awareness of their children's activities. An interventionist encouraged a 3-year-old boy by saying "tell mama that you want another sandwich and she could reach it [for you]." The mother looked at her son and said, "You do need some more. Tell Mama that you need some more tuna sandwich." He looked at her and asked, "Mom, would you get me more sandwich?"

As he reached for it, he spilled his milk, and the interventionist said in a calm, quiet voice, "Uh-oh, we've got a problem." He helped clean the table with a cloth brought to him by the interventionist. Neither staff, parents, nor children reacted to the spill, and when the milk was cleaned up, the child finished his lunch. The program staff planning meetings, the time staff spent arranging classrooms, and the parent-child lab sessions always appeared calm, well-orchestrated and well-rehearsed — despite the new families, new staff, and new students, and the turmoil the families experienced so frequently outside the program.

The parent-child labs weren't always serene, however. Although I never observed behavior from parents that was overtly verbally or physically punitive, I observed parents who issued directives and children who ignored them. One parent was said to have verbally threatened her children when she took them to use the bathroom. The most difficult time for parents and children appeared to be during outdoor play when the structure of the classroom was absent.

On one cold, rainy spring day, a regularly scheduled outdoor play period was moved to the church gym, a cavernous room with a 20' ceiling and hard surfaces that created a deafening echo from the squeal of rubber soles on tile floors and the playful shouts of children. Over a dozen wagons and riding toys were simultaneously in use by children racing in large circles around the remaining 40 or so adults and children who dodged from their paths or attempted to slow them down. The perimeter of the room had activities arranged that offered families options other than riding toys. A child-size sensory table containing potting soil, containers and shovels stood in one corner. A parent, a child, and an interventionist sat on a blanket in another corner and had a pretend picnic. Some staff and parents gathered in small groups to talk while others stooped and kneeled to converse with children. One mother, Dolores, gave her 2-year-old daughter a ride in a wagon as the child clutched her doll.

Near the end of their time together, parents and children appeared to me to move more slowly as if to make their time together last longer, knowing that they would not see each other for another long week. After awhile, they gathered toys and put them away, and some parents prepared to take their children to the child-care room before taking a cigarette break and having a debriefing of the day's session with their interventionists. CPS aides entered the gymnasium and greeted parents who had remained to ready their children to return to their foster care families. Some children left their parents and the program without obvious evidence of sorrow or care. Some children sobbed as CPS workers carried them to the state-provided vans that would transport them to their foster care homes. Dolores's 2-year-old daughter had tears trickling down her cheeks, but she did not make a sound as the CPS worker took her from her mother's arms.

PARENTS' IMPRESSIONS OF THE PARENTING PROGRAM: EARLY OPTIMISM

After their initial experiences with CPS, the Parenting Program seemed a welcome improvement to parents. They had come to the Parenting Program in several ways. Some parents, like Ann, referred themselves to the program. Some attended it because it was mandated on their service contract. Others, like Pauline, no longer had an active case with CPS, but returned to the program for support and to acquire new parenting skills that they felt they needed as their children grew and changed. A few were attending the program for the first time and attended only one 14-week session, but most families attended multiple sessions. Jean, who was required by CPS to attend the program, had been enrolled in it for more than 2 years when I met her. She held the record for the longest enrollment in the program.

What did the Parenting Program offer to counter the experiences of Jean, Ann, and Pauline and their children, and the 52 other families who attended the program that year? More than two-thirds of these parents had allegedly done things so harmful to their children that the state had removed the children from their care and placed them in foster care homes at great monetary cost to the state and great personal cost to the children and families. Was the program successful in helping families regain custody of their children, preventing future incidents of child abuse and neglect, and assuring that children lived in homes that were safe and secure and promoted their healthy growth and development?

Parents acknowledged a difference in their lives after attending the program. During interviews in which I asked parents to "tell me about the Parenting Program," without exception they shared appreciation for the skills they had acquired and the way in which they learned them, as these excerpts from three interviews illustrate.

Ann

I'm grateful to the program. The majority of the people are just there so they don't have to visit their kids in the office at CPS. They think it's stupid. But I did not have role models. I don't know. I'm trialing and erroring it here, you know? I don't know. So that's not so bad. I mean, it wasn't my fault that I didn't have good role models when I was growing up. And it's not so bad to admit that maybe I don't always know the right thing to do.

What's the big deal? I want to be, if I can be, a better person with my child. What's wrong with that? There are things that I disagree with — and that don't fit. And that's okay. But the majority of the stuff, it fits, and I've tried it, and it works.

Pauline

With everything that happened, and with Cody getting taken away and what I went through . . . the Parenting Program, I just, I don't know what I'd do without it. I really don't. Because the staff are not there to condemn you. They're not there to slap your hand. They're not there to tell you how rotten a parent you are. They know what the situation is, and they fix the situation. The people that walk out of there at the end have a lot better parenting skills. Their kids are calmed down from what they were. The parents don't have the problems that they used to.

Jean

My interventionist, she is just one in a million. I just love that lady. She's always trying to help. She doesn't only tell me what I'm doing wrong, she tells me how to get what I'm doing wrong going right. She gives me pointers [on] how to deal with it. That's what you need. It's not so much knowing what you're doing wrong. She gives me pointers how to correct what I'm doing wrong. That's what people need. I think people should be made to take a parenting class in high school. I think it should be a high school diploma kind of a thing.

Parenting classes made me understand that kids don't cry because they want to irritate you. They cry because something's wrong. They're not bad because they want to be bad. They act like they're bad because they don't know any other way. Like redirection. I never knew anything like that. It would have been so helpful. Now I know if my kids are doing something that is dangerous to them . . . something that is going to hurt them, or something that just really upsets me, I know that I can redirect them. I don't have to sit there and get totally irritated or get angry at them. I can just redirect.

I was struck by how, in the context of the program, most families and their situations seemed ordinary, and most parents appeared and felt competent. Child maltreatment seemed preventable if one talked to or even observed the parents in the program. Outside the program, however, families experienced acute or chronic crises that jeopardized the progress they made in therapeutic settings. At the outset of this study, as I observed families in the Parenting Program and listened to testimony from Pauline, Ann, and Jean, I felt hopeful about the outcomes of intervention. I had purposely refrained from gathering information about the personal histories of families except from the families themselves in an effort to avoid being influenced by others' perceptions; I believed the families themselves would show me the other sides of their stories. As the study progressed and my relationships with the three parents grew and deepened, as I observed families outside the program and parents shared confidences and explanations of how they became involved with CPS, it became increasingly difficult to remain optimistic about the eventual outcomes for families despite how intact they appeared during those 3 hours of intervention each week. Over the 2 years I conducted my research, it became more and more obvious that once in the system, it was exceedingly difficult for parents to make the lasting changes in lifestyle necessary to leave the CPS system permanently.

CHAPTER 4

IN THE SYSTEM

*I was asking for help. I was asking for help . . . but I don't think it
was the right kind of help, to take my child.*   —Ann

During the first interviews I conducted, when I asked parents to "paint
a picture" of their families, I expected parents to talk about their immediate families, especially their children. Instead, each parent spoke of
her past and of her parents. Their stories depicted childhoods of family
instability, unfinished educations, and physical and emotional maltreatment. After I listened to hours of painful family histories, I thought
about the extent to which their current lives seemed to hinge upon their
pasts. I reflected in my research log that it would have been remarkable
if they had become "good parents" with healthy, intact families.

Does this mean that child maltreatment is intergenerational and
that maltreated children are doomed to one day become parents who
maltreat their children? Not necessarily. The relationship between
abuse during childhood and subsequent parenting skills is neither linear
nor certain.

THE PERPETUATION OF CHILD MALTREATMENT

Although estimates of the percentage of intergenerational abuse
vary greatly, according to an analysis of the development of the theory
of intergenerational transmission of abusive behavior by Kaufman and
Zigler (1989), perhaps as few as one-third of people who were abused
as children become adults who abuse their children. The link between
Ann's, Jean's, and Pauline's pasts, though difficult to explain, are evident in the following descriptions of their families.

Jean

Jean's feelings about her family were mercurial. During our first
interview, Jean described her mother as "really scummy. She has head
lice. She stinks really bad." She said that for a time her mother was

living on the streets, and Jean wouldn't let her mother into her house without checking her for head lice. I interviewed Jean again, less than 2 months later, and she portrayed her mother as "dynamite with my kids. Terrific. Everything in a mother I wanted but couldn't have." It was my impression that Jean's flattering description of her mother had more to do with her need of a babysitter and her justification to me of why it was okay to leave her children in her mother's care than it did an improvement in her mother's hygiene or parenting skills.

Problems were also apparent with other family members. One sister had a baby while she was still an adolescent. She had no money and no home, so Jean told her that she would take care of her baby but that she and her "goofy little boyfriend" could not stay with Jean. She wouldn't, she explained, "subject [her] kids to . . . a change that they didn't have to go through."

Another of Jean's sisters fluctuated between being a help and being a hindrance. During the study, one of Jean's daughters was scheduled for her first overnight visit at home since she had been placed in foster care over a year before. The visit coincided with the child's 7th birthday, and Jean wanted to celebrate the occasion in her newly rented house. She hadn't received her welfare check, however, and had no means to finance the party. She explained to her daughter that they would have to celebrate her birthday the following week. Jean's sister and brother-in-law, aware of Jean's financial situation and the child's disappointment, offered to finance the party so that it could be celebrated during the child's first visit home. They spent a sum that seemed remarkably generous to Jean — more than $40.

Jean's sister — the same sister she had fought with in an alley outside the program several weeks earlier — and brother-in-law quarreled during the birthday party, then left their five children with Jean for the weekend. Another of Jean's brothers-in-law left his three children with Jean for the weekend as well. With 13 children to feed, the birthday treats soon disappeared, and Jean had to borrow $67 from a friend to buy food to feed the brood during the remainder of the weekend.

Jean's current life also involved a new boyfriend — one that spent time in and out of jail. His history included burglary "when he was younger," and drug arrests and parole violations during more recent times. He was battling a drug addiction when they met, but Jean described him as "responsible," contrasting him with the previous three men in her life who had fathered her children. He brought her gifts, including the first new bra she had owned since she left home 8 years before at the age of 14. She told me again and again how wonderful it was to have underwear that had never been worn by someone else. The

Parenting Program staff speculated as to whether the new boyfriend would mean a new baby as had previous boyfriends in Jean's life, but Jean managed to finish her 22nd year of life without giving birth to a sixth child.

Ann

Painful interactions with her parents persisted throughout Ann's life. A short time before my research began, Ann's father died unexpectedly during a trip abroad. Her mother waited a month after his death to notify Ann, telling her, "There was nothing you could have done anyway." Ann wept as she told me about a conversation with her father that occurred when she and Mike were enmeshed with CPS and had left the state with Ben.

> See, what was going on, it was me against my husband and Child Protective Services. I told my dad, "Yeah, I'm going to get custody, and I'm going to bring him home," and all that. In the meantime, Mike and I decided to get together, but we couldn't tell anybody because we didn't want Child Protective Services to know because if they would have known, they would have taken Ben from both of us.
>
> So I had to lie to my dad and tell him I was giving Mike custody. I couldn't trust my dad enough to tell him, because I was afraid he was going to tell Child Protective Services. I had to lie to him. And he was going, "Well, why all of a sudden?" because I was telling him how awful Mike was, and he's going "What is going on? Now you're just going to give up and give him custody?" So he disowned me. He said he never wanted to talk to me again, and as far as he was concerned he didn't have a daughter, and as far as I should be concerned that I don't have a father. And that was our last conversation.

Pauline

Pauline, like Ann and Jean, faced the difficult task of raising a young child alone with few resources. CPS wouldn't return Cody until Pauline found a bed and dresser for him, which seemed unobtainable on her limited income. The apartment she rented "was like a deep state of depression, it was always so dark in there . . . like a cave you had to stay in. . . . Every time I turned around, something would fall apart." Living in a place like that "has a lot to do with your life, " Pauline explained, "because everything keeps happening, and then you get to feel like nothing else is going right [either]."

Their living circumstances were difficult for Cody, too, who had no safe yard to play in or park nearby. The space was so close, and Cody was so demanding, that Pauline felt she could "barely go into the bathroom by [her]self." Pauline recalled something that Georgia had once said to her, that "sometimes it's not the parents, and it's not the children either, it's the environment." It took about 4 months for Pauline to realize that "it wasn't anything I was doing wrong, and there wasn't anything wrong with Cody. It was the environment." Pauline and her mother decided to pool their resources and find a nice place to live—a nicer place than either could afford independently. After they moved to their new apartment, Cody made a "100% turn-around." I asked her what it was about her environment that made it better. Pauline compared her new apartment with her former residence.

> There's more room. Cody has a place to go. He's always got something to do. The place looks livable, like the wires from the light switch to the light are inside the wall, you can't see them. The walls are all painted real nice. . . .
>
> I was constantly telling him he couldn't do this, and he couldn't do that because of danger. Now that he's here, he's got plenty of room, and he knows that he can only have a few toys out at a time, and then put them back and get more. Granted, that room gets to be a disaster area, but now he's got the room to play out here. He can go outside, out front on his tricycle, as long as I'm out there.

In addition to caring for Cody, Pauline cared for her mother and monitored her mother's medication. Her mother provided child care for Cody while Pauline worked or did errands. Pauline enjoyed her mother's company, and they had much in common, often riding bikes or taking walks together. Pauline likened her mother to "another kid my age running around with me." Pauline's relatively carefree relationship with her mother was transient, however. Only a few months before I conducted this study, Pauline had testified in court "against" her mother "over a commitment [by the legal and the mental health systems] to get her some treatment because she was really, really sick." Pauline's mother, who was homeless and sleeping on the streets, had begun hearing voices and was diagnosed as having schizophrenia. She was subsequently committed to a state psychiatric hospital. Although her mother's mental health seemed stable when she took medication, Pauline feared her mother's symptoms of mental illness would recur. Pauline was certain that if CPS discovered that her mother was mentally ill, they would remove Cody. Pauline was aware of the signs, and said that despite the improvement in their living situation since she and her mother began living together, her priority was Cody. If her mother's mental illness returned, Pauline told me, she would take Cody and leave rather than risk CPS taking her child a second time.

FAMILY THEORY

The important influence of relationships within families on parents and children seems evident in the parents' stories. An understanding of the relationship between family dynamics and intergenerational transmission of child maltreatment is important to the development of effective preventive approaches. Rutter (1989) explains that inadequate parenting seems to be an almost necessary, but not sufficient, condition for pervasive parenting difficulties. The outcome of child maltreatment on an individual is mediated by many factors during the interim between childhood and parenthood, including the presence of readily available and stable support systems (Egeland & Erickson, 1990; Zigler & Hall, 1989), few life stresses and healthy babies (Zigler & Hall, 1989), and foster parent or other relationships that provided emotional support to the individual as a child or adolescent (Egeland & Erickson, 1990). For the parents with whom I spoke, however, the interim between childhood and adulthood was short indeed and lacking many of the factors that make abusive behavior less likely to occur. The continuity between familial history of maltreatment and subsequent disturbances in relationships has been characterized by some researchers and theorists in two ways: the *practicing family* and the *represented family* (Main & Goldwyn, 1984; Reiss,1990).

Represented family theory attempts to explain how early relationships become internalized representations of family in the developing individual over time. The family is seen as an early context of development and relationships are believed to be constructed by dyads (e.g., mother-child) and groups of dyads (e.g., father-mother, father-child) within the context of the family. Relationships are initiated and sustained by internal structures of individual family members (Main & Goldwyn, 1984). Individual social behavior is believed to be shaped by the active, ongoing construction of an internal model of the world, and this model is the internal governor of social behavior that encourages behavioral stability and coherence across time (Reiss, 1990).

Practicing family theory states that the process of relationships results from the coordinated practices of families (Reiss, 1990). Individual internal representations of relationships are acknowledged as important, but patterns of interactions by the group are seen as paramount. Social and emotional competence is seen as part of a larger pattern of relationships. This view has been promoted by Minuchin (1974) and Reiss (1981), who believe that interactions among groups regulate and perpetuate patterns of family life. Whereas representative family theory stresses the continuity of relationships over time, according to Reiss (1990), practicing family theory emphasizes situational actions and contemporaneous fit.

The importance of these theories with regard to understanding child maltreatment and relationship disturbances centers around whether a parent's behavior toward his or her child has more to do with that parent's internal social constructs or with the social and familial milieu, and thus what kinds of interventions are needed to prevent future incidents of child maltreatment. Did the internalized personal histories of Ann, Jean, or Pauline profoundly affect their subsequent relationships with others, or are they continuing their family dance? Are there factors other than social support, relatively stress free lives, and healthy children that mediate the transmission of abusive or neglectful behavior and make the difference between the 30% of maltreated children who will become parents who maltreat their own children and the 70% who will not maltreat their children when they become parents?

THE CRIME OF POVERTY

No single factor has been identified as causing child maltreatment. Most authorities ascribe to a multivariate, process model in which a number of factors interact to determine outcomes of parenting. (See for example: Cicchetti & Rizley, 1981; Meier, 1978; Meier & Sloan, 1984.) According to Belsky (1980), child maltreatment appears to be a product of parents' histories, child temperament, social support, economic status, psychological resources, and health status. The relative contribution of these factors toward incidents of maltreatment are unknown; however, economic status is a factor frequently cited.

The majority of families who are reported to CPS for maltreating their children are poor (Pelton, 1978). One hundred percent of the parents in the program were described by the caseworkers and Parenting Program staff as poor. Less than half of the parents enrolled in the program were employed, and those who were employed at seasonal jobs or manual labor. Thirty-eight percent were unemployed and receiving public assistance. Another 13% lived with a partner who was unemployed and received public assistance. Seven parents had no source of income. A link between poverty and child maltreatment has been clearly supported by research, and this relationship exists for individual families as well as communities (Garbarino, 1990; Pelton, 1978). How does poverty contribute to child maltreatment?

Poverty typically co-occurs with a constellation of factors, all of which contribute to child maltreatment. Some factors that co-occur with poverty, such as unemployment, inadequate housing and child care, or insularity, may have transient effects. The families' stories provide concrete examples of the relationship between poverty and abuse. Pauline's description of her apartment as " . . . a deep state of depression, it was always so dark in there . . . like a cave you had to stay in" portrays the unhappiness, danger, and inconvenience of poverty. The enduring characteristics of families in poverty are more troubling.

A study conducted in England in the 1970s that examined households at or below the poverty level revealed that the majority of the children in those households were physically and emotionally maltreated and half the marriages experienced physical violence (Tonge, James, & Hillam, 1975, in Pianta, Egeland, & Erickson, 1989). The majority of the mothers in this study were inconsistent and punitive in their approach to discipline. Their homes were disorganized (meals were unplanned, and work, school, and daily routines were absent) and children often went unsupervised.

Jean's house exemplifies these conditions, as did her description of her parenting during the time her children were removed by CPS: "I didn't care if my house was clean. I didn't care if my kids were clean. I didn't care if they breathed, much less anything else . . . I used to pull [my daughter] around by the hair. I used to slug her."

Although Jean appeared to have learned alternatives to physical maltreatment and ways to interact more positively with her children, the caregiving environment she provided her children was far from optimal. During my first visit to a newly rented house that Jean obtained at a reduced rate through the Federal Section VIII Housing Subsidy Program, I recorded in my field notes that the house had "wall-to-wall carpeting, high ceilings with coving, fresh paint, a fireplace, built-in cabinets in the dining area with beautiful glass knobs and glass doors." It was, Jean said, "the nicest place I ever lived." On subsequent visits, the house was cluttered, the children ate cookies for breakfast, the front door was open and half-clothed, dirty children were out on the lawn, and Jean's daughter was at home rather than attending school. On one of those visits, Jean's eldest daughter, who was 7, described how she had made her mother a cake for Mother's Day.

> *Child*: I made it by myself.
> *Jean*: They got to mix it by themselves and put the ingredients in by themselves. . . .
> *Child*: My mom was asleep.
> *Jean*: No I wasn't. I was in the kitchen watching . . .
> *Child*: Oh yeah. You were in the kitchen watching us.

Later in our conversation, Jean described her boyfriend's merits as her infant daughter wailed from the next room. She seemed not to hear her child's cries as she described how "terrific" her boyfriend was with her children, then read a poem she wrote about her daughters. As she read it, her 7-year-old daughter whispered the words in chorus.

> Little girls are good, as long as they're never misunderstood.
> Frilly little dresses, long curly hair,
> Never ending smiles to be messed with only if you should dare.
> So pure and unassured everything is going on around them.
> Their only fear is the adults of the world that are going to hurt them.
> Four lovely girls born onto me, to love, honor and care for.
> God gave them to me.

Jean's daughter announced that she also wrote a poem and explained that she only wrote one poem because her mother wouldn't give her a second piece of paper. Jean read the poem her 7-year-old daughter wrote about her boyfriend, while the daughter listened and corrected her.

> Me and you put together as a perfect couple.
> And when I put my arms out and you hug me, I suddenly start to melt.

Jean did not question the appropriateness of the poem's content for a child of 7, but during a subsequent conversation she expressed concern that her daughter had no friends her own age, that her friends were 15, 16, and 17 years of age. Jean tried "to take every adult thing away. I don't let her curl her hair no more. I don't let her put on makeup. I don't let her cook. I do not let her care for the kids. I've taken every adult thing I know, even drinking coffee. That's an adult social thing that adults do." It seemed to me that Jean had listened to the words of caseworkers and interventionists who I knew expressed concerns in private about the child's adultlike behavior. One couldn't be certain that Jean's actions matched her words when others were not around, but staff members suspected that Jean's current parenting behavior was consistent with her past parenting behavior.

Besides relying on her mother for child care, Jean left her daughter with a man and woman who had previously been involved with CPS because the man had been accused of sexually abusing his girlfriend's developmentally delayed daughter. Jean reasoned the couple "had to be good parents. CPS gave their kids back, and they do a background check and all this." In fact, Georgia was uneasy about this couple, but because she did not have any hard evidence, it would have been unethical to warn Jean about them by offering information that might be slanderous. Instead Georgia urged Jean to never leave her children with anyone she did not know very well. Jean "kept seeing [her daughter] not wanting to stay with them," but said she was "so excited about getting this house," that she "really didn't think much about it." One evening when Jean went dancing to celebrate renting her house and leaving the shelter, she left her 8-year-old daughter in the care of the couple her daughter feared. The child was sodomized while in their care.

Jean says her daughter is "really tough. She's streetwise . . . knows about drugs, and has already tried smoking." Jean can "tell [by] how she carries herself, she's going to be really a problem child. . . . It scares the death" out of Jean. Jean wants her children to "grow up and go to college and have the best of things." Jean purports to believe — although there is considerable evidence that she is frequently dishonest, at least with herself — that every mother wants the best for her children. Jean reasons that because of her children's experiences she has "to exercise more concern and help [her] children [more] than the regular parent would have to, and," she adds one caveat, "that's hard."

Although the inadequate parenting skills typified by Jean are not evidenced in most families that live in poverty, they are more prevalent in poor families than in middle class families. Maltreatment of children is a pervasive, persistent problem of interaction within caregiving environments that interferes with children's healthy development (Erickson, Egeland, & Pianta, 1989), and appears to have damaging effects beyond those of poverty alone, such as cognitive and social-emotional delays and disorders in children (Egeland & Erickson, 1987; Egeland & Sroufe, 1981; Egeland, Sroufe, & Erickson, 1983). Although the incidence of children with developmental delays or disabilities between the ages of birth and 6 years ranges from approximately 2% to 12% in the general population, approximately 15% of children enrolled in the Parenting Program had confirmed developmental delays, and the developmental status of another 18% was in question. The continuing rise of poverty in combination with parents who themselves have tragic histories and few personal and social resources — to address the demands of parenting children with special health and developmental needs — places families in double jeopardy and presents a dismal forecast given the current economic and societal trends. It appears that we are continuing a trend started at least a decade ago, a decade most unkind to the growing number of children and families living in poverty in our nation.

Despite ranking second in the world in per capita gross national product, the United States does not compare favorably with other industrialized nations in measures of children's health and well-being. According to the Children's Defense Fund (1990), the United States ranked 19th in infant mortality, 22nd in the mortality rate for children under 5 years of age, 29th in low birth-weight babies, and 15th in the proportion of 1-year-old children who are fully immunized against polio. The United States had the highest percentage of children living in poverty of eight industrialized nations. The poverty rate among children in our country was 2 to 3 times that of most other countries studied (Children's Defense Fund, 1990).

The proportion of children living in poverty in America grew 23% between 1979 and 1988 (Children's Defense Fund, 1990), and ranged from 14.7% of white children and 37.4% of Hispanic children to 43.6% of African-American children in 1990 (Annie E. Casey Foundation, 1992). Poverty, like child maltreatment, is highest among families headed by women and families headed by someone younger than 25 years of age (Children's Defense Fund, 1990).

According to a 1988 report from the Center on Budget and Policy Priorities in which poverty programs and policies in America were examined, the 1980s brought a high level of economic recovery; however, an unusually high poverty rate (13.6%) persisted (Shapiro & Greenstein, 1988). The safety nets for people living in poverty, such as Medicaid and WIC, differ from state to state with respect to adequacy of funding, quality, and accessibility to families, but no state in our nation has constructed a net without holes. According to the report, "In thirty-two states, the maximum Aid to Families with Dependent Children (AFDC) cash benefit for a family of three with no other income is below fifty percent of the poverty line. In nine states, these benefits are less than one-third of the poverty line" (p. 1). This translates to $603 per month for a family of three in Vermont in 1987. In contrast, the maximum benefit for a family of three in Alabama was $118 per month in 1987. In Alabama, the maximum benefit was 15.6% of the 1987 figures for income at the poverty line, and in Vermont it was 79.8% of the 1987 figures for income at the poverty line (Shapiro & Greenstein, 1988). In neither state were the benefits sufficient to feed, clothe, house, educate, and purchase health care for a family of three.

What are the consequences of poverty? "Poor children are more likely to die in infancy, be disabled for life by preventable causes, lack basic reading and math skills, drop out of school, be unemployed, become pregnant as teenagers, and be dependent on welfare" (Children's Defense Fund, 1990). Poverty is damaging in and of itself, regardless of whether children are also exposed to maltreatment (Elmer, 1977). A study conducted at the University of Washington by the Washington Children's Health Research and Policy Group used a Delphi research approach to survey and distill expert judgments from 90 doctors, teachers, program administrators and community representatives who were knowledgeable about children's issues. They concluded that children's problems in all areas are much more interdependent than current policy acknowledges, and that for the most part those problems seem to be related to poverty "in the richest nation on the globe" (Schwendiman & Porter, 1990).

One of the family interventionists in the Parenting Program expressed her frustration about the situations related to poverty that were faced by the parents with whom she worked.

As my brother always says when I'm complaining about some issue or another—you know, when a family's had a really hard time or when I'm angry because a child is homeless—my brother will say in a very sarcastic tone, 'Yes, but they are our most important resource.' Lip service is basically what it is. I mean, there's one statistic that shoots the theory all to hell, [the theory] that the bottom line is the best interest of the child, and that's that children are the number one, fastest growing population of poor in the country. . . . That's abuse as a matter of public policy. That's the worst kind of abuse. It's the most insidious, and it's the most frustrating, and [it] makes me angrier than anything. It makes it really hard for me to get angry at a parent. It's sort of picking on the little guy, the defenseless guy, to go after parents when society can allow a child to be living under those conditions.

Eight families in the program were homeless, and another 14 lived in housing that was dirty, crowded, unstable, and unsafe. Some lived in temporary shelters for the homeless. One mother lived in a single motel room with her brother and five children. Other problems seemed less serious, but wore on families. Parents and children lacked dental care, and there wasn't a time during my study when at least one parent was not experiencing pain from an abscessed tooth. Medical coupons would pay to have teeth pulled, but not filled. Transportation was necessary but not affordable. Parents lacked the education, training, and social savvy necessary to obtain jobs that yielded more than government subsidies provided.

Given the complexity of the situations in which maltreatment occurred and the multiple, severe, and chronic problems families in the program faced, as well as the influence of the personal histories of the parents on their current behavior, how effective were CPS and the Parenting Program able to be in treating and preventing future occurrences of child maltreatment?

There was little agreement or common understanding among families and staff about CPS's reason for being. The concepts of "abuse and neglect" were ambiguous to all involved. Most agreed that some kind of intervention was needed, but there was little agreement about which kind of intervention was the right intervention. Uncertainty about the mission of CPS and the types of interventions it employs to address incidents of child maltreatment are not unique to this study; rather, it pervades the child welfare system in our country.

IN THE CHILD'S BEST INTEREST

Foster care was one of the primary interventions used by CPS, and staff at the Parenting Program were particularly skeptical about its efficacy in reducing incidents of maltreatment or addressing conditions that contribute to incidents of maltreatment. They expressed concern about the impact of foster care on children. This attitude is clearly conveyed in the following excerpt from an interview with one of the interventionists in the program:

It doesn't work. I mean, obviously it doesn't work. If it worked, there would be fewer and fewer children in foster care; less and less need. If it worked, children would go into a foster home, if it was absolutely necessary, and they would be in one foster home until they were removed to return to their parents. Instead they go through 10 or 12 over the course of a few years — 2 or 3 years. To have a child removed from the home that long, it's just ridiculous, it's unnecessary. There needs to be a decision made one way or the other for the child, but to keep a child in limbo — especially when they're so young [is wrong].

The other thing that happens is that they remove young children who are so vulnerable, who don't understand that they're not at fault, that they haven't done anything wrong, [or why] they're the ones who are punished. Yet, the state is supposed to [act in] the best interest of the child. Well, certainly, if the child is in danger, but I think more often than not they don't stand back and evaluate the situation real carefully and decide [whether removal of the child] is really necessary, because this child, who we're supposed to be protecting, is the person who is going to be the most vulnerable and the most affected by our decision. If people could just put themselves back [in time] and think of how they would feel as a young child — [being] taken away from their parents. How frightening! What's the most frightening thing of all that can happen to you as a child? That would be it.

The notion that legal intervention in families and foster care placements are effective in preventing the maltreatment of children is not supported by empirical evidence. For example, half of the children who died from abuse or neglect in New York City during one 6-month period lived in families who had already been reported to the child welfare agency (Mayor's Task Force on Child Abuse and Neglect, 1983). Of the 55 parents who participated in the Parenting Program during the year this study was conducted, 28 had previously been involved with CPS and 5 parents had previously relinquished their parental rights or had their parental rights terminated. Removal of children from their homes in and of itself does not resolve the problems associated with maltreatment; removal is part of a extended process that may or may not lead to favorable outcomes for children.

Once removed from homes considered to be dangerous, children may suffer maltreatment while in foster care placements. This concern was frequently expressed by staff in the Parenting Program. The first day I observed the program, one of the staff of the program who had been given work space at the CPS office told colleagues that CPS was "in crisis" because there were so many children who needed foster care placements and there were not sufficient foster care homes available for them. She spoke of two children in the program, 2 and 4 years of age, who had lived in 5 different foster care homes during their short lives. Their current foster family had wanted an infant, so they agreed to take the 4-year-old in order to raise his younger sister, but the placement wasn't working out.

Staff who had visited the two children in their foster home expressed dismay about the differential treatment of the children by the foster parents, who provided toys for one child and displayed photos of her like "shrines" while her brother had "only a bed and dresser . . . with the drawers turned toward the walls," thus making them inaccessible to him. One staff member said that CPS would never again place children with this foster family because the care they provided was so inadequate. Another staff member commented that the case had been in limbo for a long time, and because they did not have another available placement for the children, CPS was going to return the children to their biological mother to see "how she does." If she failed, CPS would begin the process of terminating the mother's parental rights. The Parenting Program staff believed that at that time she would probably fail. I wondered where the children would go then.

Each passing week in the Parenting Program seemed to bring a new crisis in a child's life. Co-director Georgia pulled me aside during one session to tell me that Jean's 5-year-old daughter may have been sexually abused by another child in her foster home. I passed Jean's small figure sitting alone on the floor of the long, dimly lit church corridor, hugging her knees to her chest, weeping. At the time, Jean was living in a single room in a shelter for homeless families with three of her five children. One of her sons and one of her daughters remained in foster care, Jean said, because CPS believed she did not have enough room at the shelter for all five of her children. At least, Jean told me, her children wouldn't be "molested" in the shelter. Georgia telephoned Jean's caseworker, who promptly arrived at the program to talk to the child. The caseworker told Jean that none of the children in that foster home would return there that day. It wasn't clear where they would go when the session ended in a few hours.

Decisions abruptly made during times of crisis left no opportunity to prepare children and parents for traumatic separations. The staff believed that the disruption of relationships between parents and children that occurred when children were placed in foster care had an impact on the developing child. Isabelle described the reunions and separations of parents and children as they arrived and departed the Parenting Program as being a source of "extreme pain for both the child and the parent." But even when the parent and child were permanently reunited, relationships were difficult to repair and rebuild. When their children remained in foster homes for protracted periods, parents discovered "they no longer knew their child like they used to." Parents expressed dismay about their children's behavior when they returned from foster care placements, and Isabelle would explain to parents that being removed from home was "as extreme a trauma for children as for parents if one considered the child's perspective . . . and the fear of losing you again, even though they might not be able to verbalize it, would certainly affect their behavior."

Georgia expressed concern about the use of foster care as an intervention for child maltreatment and about its effects on children.

Susan: Can you see an impact on the children?

Georgia: Yes.

Susan: What kinds of things do you see?

Georgia: Well, this is difficult because I can't figure out how descriptive I should be or how objective I should be . . . I see behaviors, and I attribute them to certain things. It looks like we have children who aren't really attaching to anybody. I've seen one child who was physically abused in two foster homes. She went to foster care when she was 6 months old for failure to thrive. Her mother was drug addicted. And the first foster home she went to was overcrowded because there was a shortage of [foster homes], and she was laid in a crib all the time. Then pretty soon she started learning how to climb and so forth. Anyway, she apparently disturbed her foster mother, and she was jerked by the leg. We don't know how it happened, but she ended up with a spinal fracture, and the doctors were pretty clear that it was not an accident, that someone had done this to her. Then she went from there to another home where they had this big huge dog, and the dog bit the child, and left a real large mark on her face. We told the foster parent that the dog had to go, and she said, "No, you take the kid." The child ended up in I don't know how many foster care placements, and she has now gone home after many, many placements, but she doesn't seem to be too attached to people . . . not terribly interested in them.

I see that happening a lot. I see a lot of behavior problems with kids. A kid I know now has been in nine foster homes in a year, and he's considered a behavior problem. One of the reasons he has been kicked out of all the foster homes is they think he's so obnoxious. We've never seen the behavior that the foster parents talk about. I worked with this kid nearly a year. I've never seen it. But they say that his behavior is really out of control, that he's aggressive and mean to the other children. I don't see it, but I imagine he's so use to rejection that it could be he's setting them up in his foster homes for them to reject him. Who knows what he's doing?

Susan: How old is he?

Georgia: Three. He's really targeted as a bad kid. I think children in foster care can't help but thinking that they're responsible. I know that a lot of them feel that they created [the situation they are in]. A child went up to me and said, "I want you to know that I really did run out of the house when Mom spanked me. And they put me in foster care, and it was really my fault, so can I go home now?" He must have felt that he was a really bad kid . . . and of course they would. How else do children explain things that happen to them?

The consequences of multiple, extended foster care placements are seen not only in the immediate behavior of young children. There may be long-term consequences for those children who enter and reenter what has been called the "revolving door" of the foster care system. The effects of foster care may also be reflected in the disproportionate number of homeless young people in our nation who, having exited the foster care system at age 18, are without the "money, skills, or family support to make it on their own" (Barden, 1991).

Oddly enough, Fanshel and Shinn (1978) did not find evidence from their 5-year study of children in foster care that foster care placements had a detrimental effect on the intellectual or psychosocial development of children. It is difficult to access the thoughts of the children and gauge their perceptions of foster care. Perhaps children's feelings about their parents are ambivalent. One cannot be certain because young children may not be able to articulate their feelings, and because the recollections of adults who lived in foster care placements during childhood is mediated by subsequent experience. But more than once during this study, as I observed children who were returned to their parents, or removed from their parents, or who remained in limbo, my thoughts were akin to those of a public health nurse who spoke about children of alcoholics in *The Broken Cord* (Dorris, 1989).

You have to remember that children here know or see only one way of life. This is the way that they've grown up. They *like* their parents. Hard as that may seem to some people to accept, this is their mom and their dad, and they love them. And just as hard as it may be for some people to accept, mothers and dads love their kids. You can't make the judgment that they don't care (p. 193).

The staff of the Parenting Program also believed that parents cared about their children, and the notion that families who maltreat their children are worth preserving persisted among them. Public sentiment and social policies and practices that promoted legal intervention, foster care, and adoption, despite a lack of evidence of their effectiveness in preventing child maltreatment, added to the conflict felt by parents and staff about the role CPS should play in preventing child maltreatment.

THE FUNCTIONS OF CHILD PROTECTIVE SERVICES

Counter to my expectations when I began this study, every parent believed that CPS should have intervened in their parenting on behalf of their children. There was ambivalence about the kind of intervention CPS should have employed, however, and during the interview in which Ann made the statement, "I don't think it was the right kind of help, to take my child," she reversed her position several times regarding what she believed to be the most appropriate treatment, stopping at one point to say, "Wait, I'm contradicting myself." Ann's insight into the CPS caseworker's decision about removing Ben is apparent in this excerpt from an interview:

[The caseworker] made a comment to my mother-in-law's room- mate, before she took him, that Ben didn't look like he was abused. But when the caseworker looked at the whole picture, there's a restraining order, there's drinking going on, there's abuse . . . The caseworker really didn't [have a choice]. I don't think that it could have been avoided.

Ann seemed to acknowledge that the parenting she and her hus- band provided for their son was questionable enough to warrant his removal by CPS. But could Ben's removal from home have been avoided? An alternative to child removal and subsequent foster care or adoption is family preservation. Rhetoric about family preservation has prevailed throughout the 1990s, but child welfare agencies "have traditionally been little other than foster care agencies" in terms of function and allocation of resources (Pelton, 1990). The function of the

CPS agency in this study, in accordance with legislation and policy, was "to prevent further abuse, safeguard and enhance the welfare of abused children, and preserve family life when consistent with the protection of the child by stabilizing the family and improving parental capacity. . . ." One of the primary strategies used by CPS to deliver services to accomplish that purpose was the service contract with the family that was developed when child maltreatment was initially substantiated and a CPS case was opened.

Service contracts list a number of requirements that parents must fulfill before children can be returned or a case can be closed. Although it is crucial to the resolution of CPS cases, some parents in the program could not identify the purpose of the service contract, and others were unaware that they had a contract. Fulfilling such a contract does not guarantee parents the return of their children or that their cases will be closed, and moreover, the services listed on contracts do not guarantee their availability. Service contracts might prescribe such varied services as drug or alcohol treatment programs, clean random UAs (no presence of drugs or alcohol in unscheduled urine assays), anger management classes, behavior management classes, homemaker visits, or on-time attendance for parent-child visits. Although service contracts were developed for individual families, limited options for services within the agency and community made contracts among families more alike than different, and contracts never addressed issues associated with poverty. Some families did not know what service contracts were after months of involvement with CPS, and some were unaware that they had a contract with CPS. Others simply "slipped through the cracks."

One mother in the Parenting Program who had moved from another state with her husband, two children, and an active CPS case, had never met her caseworker during the first year following her move. A year after the family relocated, the father lost his job, money grew scarce, and tension increased. A violent dispute erupted between the couple, and the mother took her sons to a babysitter to remove them from the situation. She hardly knew the babysitter but knew no one else who would care for her children. While at the babysitter's, the 2-year-old fell off a bunk bed and broke his leg. The child went without treatment for 24 hours, so the story went, because the babysitter did not know how to contact the parents. (The babysitter did not know the family's last name, and they did not have a telephone.) The mother retrieved her children the following day and headed for the emergency room.

The CPS caseworker met her in the emergency waiting room at the hospital and scrawled a service contract on a piece of scrap paper while the child's leg was being set with the first of a series of casts. Because the mother had already voluntarily completed most of the standard requirements enumerated on the service contract (she had self-referred to the Parenting Program and attended each week), the caseworker, who shared the service contract with the family's Parenting Program interventionist and admitted that he was embarrassed by the situation, recommended case closure before the child's cast was removed and his leg healed. Case closure meant not only the end of monitoring the children's safety and development (and both children had significant developmental problems), it meant the end of services and transportation to intervention supported by CPS. Those services were available only to families currently involved with the CPS System, not to prevent future involvement with CPS or to address the specific needs of children and families.

Service contracts and many of the interventions they prescribed seemed to have little credibility with some families, and they were perceived as having little impact on the situations surrounding families involved with CPS. Homemaker visits were sometimes prescribed to assist families in managing daily household duties such as cleaning and cooking, but parents' perceptions of their purpose differed from that of CPS as evidenced by Pauline's description of the homemaker visits she received.

> She ordered me a homemaker right the week that I got Cody back. That lady came to my house one day. She seen how well I was doing, and she came back. She was supposed to be there 6 hours a week, 2 hours Monday, Wednesday, and Friday. Every single time she came over, alls we did was sit there and shoot the breeze. All we did, we sat there and gabbed and gabbed and gabbed — just like two old hens. She'd bring me a recipe, and I'd send her a recipe just like any other friend. She'd come over and we'd sit and gab and yeah, this is going on and this is going on and this is the new hot gossip this week. And that was it. Finally I got to the point where I went in, and I told my caseworker, "Look, my release for me to go to work is up, and I want to go to work. I need to go to work. I have to have more income." I mean, that's flat out how it was. I went and told her, "Look, she's in my way." So finally I had to get rid of her before I could get my case closed.

One afternoon as I observed the program, one of the family interventionists told a parent that CPS didn't have enough money to purchase bus tokens to transport families to the Parenting Program that month. The parent commented that CPS could save a lot of money by not paying for homemaker services. She didn't know, she said, "what sitting around and talking has to do with homemaking," and expressed the belief that homemakers were "spies to see how your kids are." Assignment of homemakers to parents involved with CPS was perhaps in part a response to this need, but parents seemed unclear about the purpose of the visits, saw them as a "waste of time," and viewed home visitors as presenting a nuisance or even as "spies." If visits from homemakers were effective in providing support or reducing stress, it was not verbally acknowledged by the parents to whom I spoke.

The demands CPS placed on parents in order to have children returned to their homes seemed nonsensical to Pauline as well, who said that by the time Cody was returned, she had "taken every single class they have twice . . . the underlying causes of abuse, anger management, behavior management, and the Parenting Program." Pauline valued some of the classes she took from CPS, but felt manipulated by the demands CPS levied.

> *Pauline*: I don't know how to describe those people down there at CPS, but they're crazy. They really are. And I wish someone would put a stop to the stupid malarkey that they're pulling . . . they took my kid away because I was only 17 years old. Now is that a real reason to take your kid away? . . . CPS really, in some ways, did some damage to me because of all the mental anguish I had to go through, and the frustration is the worst part of it. The waiting, and everything else. The wondering. How long it going to be? Am I going to be fighting for 2 years and then end up losing my kid because of the stupid [rules]? I swear, they could find a rule for everything.
>
> *Susan*: How did you figure out what was going on? When you got yourself in that situation, how did you figure out what you needed to do?
>
> *Pauline*: They told me there was certain things I need to do, like go back to school, take these classes. The first think I learned was not to fight them.
>
> *Susan*: How did you learn that?
>
> *Pauline*: I went to my caseworker the first time I ever seen her and cussed her out, and I found out that they took visitations away because of that. They prolonged my visitation.
>
> *Susan*: Prolonged your visitation. [Do you mean they] prolonged the time between [your] visits [with Cody]?

> *Pauline*: Yeah. It was like 2 weeks [between visits with Cody],
> then it was [changed to] 3 or 4 weeks.

Some services offered by CPS were valued by parents and were perceived as useful. A class that addressed the foundations of abuse in the personal histories of parents was mentioned by Ann, Pauline, and Jean as helpful to them in recognizing the influence of their pasts on their current behavior. However, it wasn't until parents reached the Parenting Program that they began to gain confidence in their abilities to parent, and by the time they reached the program, it was late in the game. Their children had already been removed, and some had been in foster care for protracted periods of time.

PARENTS AND CPS: THEM AND US

A cogent model of therapeutic intervention was not apparent as I observed parents' interactions with the child welfare system. Treatment approaches, one could reasonably argue, should correspond to and address the causes and correlates of child maltreatment. Instead, CPS intervention seemed to encourage labeling of adults who maltreat their children, what Zigler and Hall (1989) have referred to as a "them" and "us" approach. One result of this approach was that parents were seen as deviant and as agents separate from the contexts of family, culture, and society. A second result was that parents' relationships with CPS became adversarial rather than therapeutic, as Isabelle's description of parents' reactions to CPS portray:

> I think that people are very afraid of CPS. They see them as having the ultimate power. They don't see them as a help in their case; they see them as the enemy. They don't feel that they can be honest. I think that's why lots of times they lie, because CPS is involved in their lives in a way that they feel very uncomfortable with.

Pauline described an unexpected meeting with her CPS caseworker that occurred in her neighborhood grocery store. Cody had already been returned to her custody, and her case had been closed, but Pauline's apprehension and distrust of CPS remained.

> I was so nervous when my caseworker came over here. We had just moved in the first of this month. We got moved in on the

third, and my caseworker came over on the 5th, the 6th . . . My case was already closed. I ran into her up here at [the grocery store] . . . Of course I don't have nothing to hide from her. The only thing is that I feel a threat because of my mom being with me and around Cody. I was so nervous when my caseworker was here, I was stuttering. That's how nervous I was. I haven't heard nothing from them or anything. But it's just—I know CPS can get away with a lot of things. . . . [When Cody was in foster care] I almost got involved with [an advocacy group for parents involved with CPS], then I got thinking, 'great, this is all I need.' If I started problems with CPS, it would be a long time before I got my kid back, so I just dropped them completely. I was so nervous that I was stuttering.

It could be assumed that if parents were seen as deviant or disturbed, psychotherapy or counseling would serve as the cornerstone of therapeutic intervention and would be readily available. However, psychological services appeared to be limited to documentation of the psychological status of parents, usually at the request of CPS, rather than therapeutic intervention. More than a year after her initial involvement with CPS, Ann found that the therapeutic services to address the psychological problems that were so carefully documented by CPS remained difficult to obtain.

Ann: I'm willing to admit that there is a potential for abuse, you know, and there is a problem.

Susan: Are you getting help?

Ann: No, and that's what gripes me about the system. It's like everything is court ordered, and we can't afford it. And I've made that known to Child Protective Services, and they don't have any services available within Child Protective Services to help. I mean, I have been . . . crying out for help. . . . Like I've told my caseworker, 'When are you going to get the counseling? Things are getting bad. When are you going to get the counseling?' 'Well, you're on the waiting list, You'll get there, just hang in there.' Hang in there? It's like, it's getting bad, it's getting bad. Oh, okay, now we're separated. You know? Shit hit the fan, and now we're separated, and there's a big crisis. Now do we get some help? 'No, you're still on the waiting list.'

The contribution of stress in precipitating incidents of child maltreatment has been described by many researchers (see for example: Gil, 1970; Kempe & Kempe, 1978; Garbarino, 1976; Meier & Sloan,

1984), yet it seemed to be disregarded in the design of interventions for the families involved with CPS, in spite of the stream of changes and misfortunes that the parents experienced during the brief time I knew them.

For example, during the initial 4 months I collected data in the Parenting Program, Jean brawled with her sister, reconciled with her, then borrowed money from her to celebrate her daughter's 7th birthday and first homecoming after 2 years in foster care. She learned that the same daughter may have been sexually abused in foster care, and that her 8-year-old daughter was sodomized by a man to whom Jean had entrusted her care. She appeared in court to provide testimony about the man who abused her daughter, moved from sheltered housing into her own apartment, and was separated from her boyfriend when he was arrested. More than needing someone to help her deal with life's stresses, Jean, and other parents in the program, needed to learn ways to avoid creating or encountering situations in which stress was inherent.

Treatment approaches that focus on the link between actions and thoughts, the encouragement of thoughtful action, and the reduction of impulsive acts may be found in the literature on child maltreatment. (See Newberger & Cook, 1983; Egeland, Olds, & Musick, 1991.) There was sporadic use of intervention strategies that were suggestive of this in the Parenting Program. Active problem solving was used during didactic training sessions, and collaborative goal setting and self evaluation of progress toward goals occurred in large groups and one on one with parents and interventionists during weekly sessions. Parents were encouraged to identify problems and issues in their lives, to generate possible solutions, and to anticipate what might occur if they acted on their ideas. During the program, time was allocated following parent-child labs for the parents and staff to sit on couches and comfortable chairs in a large group and review the progress made that day toward their individual goals and discuss events that had occurred during the parent-child labs and the previous week.

This approach emphasized the relationship between the parents' thoughts and actions and promoted the idea that the parents had some control over the events in their lives. The approach was based on an assumption that events outside the immediate relationship between parent and child were powerful mediators of parent-child relationships, and it viewed relationships between parents and children as dynamic and changeable over time, demanding constantly changing skills from parents as children experienced developmental changes. The Parenting Program attempted to provide intervention that was flexible, according to family situations that would likely change from week to week, however, the program was not available to families during the time relationships between parents and children were first established.

THINGS MUST FALL APART

Recent research conducted by Egeland and Erickson (1990) indicates that the "transition to parenthood is a ripe time for therapeutic intervention with young women with a history of being maltreated — a time to help them come to grips with their past and hopefully, to take steps toward breaking the intergenerational cycle of abuse and neglect" (p. 29). But the Parenting Program was unavailable to most parents who were under CPS jurisdiction, and the stress and disruption that typically accompanies parenthood (Cowan & Cowan, 1989, in Egeland & Erickson, 1990) — and was so evident in Jean's, Pauline's, and Ann's lives — goes largely unaddressed because support and therapeutic intervention are unavailable or inaccessible to more and more parents in this country, especially during the critical time when they first become parents. The unwritten rule seems to be: In order to get services, things must first fall apart. And even when things fall apart, there are no guarantees that families will get anything they needed.

Complex factors, including the personal histories of parents and children, their developmental functioning, their feelings and attitudes, and their mental and physical health often were not considered when CPS planned intervention. The continuous, reciprocal interplay between the changing, growing child and the changing physical and social environment that defines the transactional model hypothesized by Sameroff and Chandler (1975) was not addressed by intervention that was early, continuous, or flexible. The contexts of extended family and community that influence incidents of child maltreatment, such as isolation and lack of familial support systems (factors that are prevalent in research about parents who maltreat their children, and were common among parents in the Parenting Program), as well as economic hardship and the loss of esteem by self and others that accompanies unemployment and underemployment in a society that values and conspicuously displays its wealth (Garbarino, 1990) were overlooked, and worse, were sometimes seen as personal shortcomings of the parents. Societal policies, practices, attitudes, and expectations, for example, the expectation and mandate that parents must not harm their children, were at odds with the society experienced by most families in the program. The cultural milieu of the families in the Parenting Program, like more and more families in our country, was characterized by violence and a reliance on aggression for solving problems, with corporal punishment used as a fundamental means of discipline. One wonders how parents, particularly those with cognitive impairments or those who never experienced gentleness, consideration, and orderliness from their families or society, could make distinctions between permissible and impermissible physical and emotional punishment. A comment of Ann's led me to believe that parents may doubt the integrity of messages that are clearly discrepant with actual child rearing practices in our country, or at least with practices in the subcultures of some parents.

> You know, if they're going to be so critical and judgmental of me then they can come and raise my son, if they think they can do a better job than I can. And it turns out that they go home and spank their children too. You can't tell me that the workers, that work in Child Protective Services, if their kid was biting, they wouldn't spank him. You can't tell me that. [One of the interventionists] told me her boy bit her, and she just walked away. And I'm sitting there going, "Yeah, I know you can't tell me what you really did."

The lack of consistency between customary parenting practices and expectations for parents by the child welfare system, and the lack of a coherent conceptual model employed by the child welfare system, were apparent in the patchwork of interventions offered or coordinated by CPS. A clear map leading parents and caseworkers to accomplish the goal of CPS "to prevent further abuse, safeguard and enhance the welfare of abused children, and preserve family life when consistent with the protection of the child by stabilizing the family and improving parental capacity"[3] was lacking.

Parenting Program staff, although not always able to provide everything they thought parents and children needed, were articulate about what they believed they should do and were clear about their philosophies and the rationales underlying the therapeutic approach they employed. Parents were equally articulate about what they liked and disliked about the system, and what they believed worked and did not work in the Parenting Program. The staff spent hours planning and debriefing meetings, building close relationships with families, and considering the feedback provided to them from evaluations of parents' satisfaction with the program. These efforts combined to create an approach to intervention with families that was quite unlike any intervention families had previously experienced in the child welfare system.

---

[3]A citation for this quote was omitted in order to protect the identify of the parents, program, and program staff represented in this book.

CHAPTER 5

SUPPORTING, REPARENTING, AND EMPOWERING

Although each parent, staff member, and CPS worker understood the Parenting Program from a unique perspective, there was remarkable consistency among staff and parents in their sense of the program's philosophy, purposes, and strengths. Every staff person mentioned that one of the program's greatest merits was that it changed in response to families' perceptions of their needs, new research findings about effective intervention methodologies, and staff perceptions of families' needs. The parents and staff had common understandings about the principal purposes of the program, the unwritten rules that governed the system, and the relationships of parents and staff within the system.

PARENT AND PROFESSIONAL RELATIONSHIPS

Isabelle believed that the collaboration between the Community Program and CPS helped make the Parenting Program successful. The program staff mentioned that access to multiple perspectives from both agencies—knowledge of parent training techniques, behavior management and problem solving skills from CPS parent trainers, and knowledge of children and their development from the Community Program staff—contributed to effective intervention with families. Although differences between co-workers contributed to the success of the Parenting Program, differences between agencies made collaboration challenging at times.

A difference in the focus and purpose of the Parenting Program and CPS was mentioned by the parents and staff. It was a difference that seemed simultaneously a strength and a source of contention, as this interview with Isabelle illustrates.

> *Isabelle*: I would say [one difference between the Parenting Program and CPS is] that we aren't really investigating these families. We monitor, but we aren't the ones deciding if they should

get their kids back. We aren't the court. We aren't the workers going to the court, and I think that's what helps to balance the program. The parents are already nervous because they're a part of Child Protective Services. And when they come to a program, and it's sponsored by CPS, it has to be defined, who we are, and how we operate, and what the rules are. Yes, we will report any situation [of abuse]. I think it's only right that parents know what their rights are. I get disturbed if we don't let parents know what will happen, how it works, how the system works, what our goal is.

Susan: Do they come in not knowing sometimes?

Isabelle: Oh, I don't think people know at all when they come. We have to orient them extensively, and I think even after orienting them, some of the people I was talking about really don't adapt to this particular parent training program, I don't think they ever really understand, ever feel comfortable. They always feel like they're being watched by CPS, the big, bad monster out there.

Susan: So you think [that is] parents' perceptions of CPS—not all parents it sounds like—but some parents really have that perception?

Isabelle: I think they have a real escalated—how can I put this? I think that people are very afraid of CPS. They see them as having the ultimate power. They don't see them as a help in their case, they see them as the enemy. They don't feel that they can be honest. I think that's why lots of times they lie, because CPS is involved in their lives in a way that they feel very uncomfortable with. I don't think that they have a trust relationship in most cases with their caseworkers. I think there are some that do.

I had a mom recently who was in a situation in the program where there was a lot of withholding of information or lying going on between herself and her interventionist. And at one point I talked with her about it, and I just said, "You know, if this is going to work for you, if it's going to work for me, and if it's going to work for your child, we've got to be honest. And I don't really feel like expending any more of my energy to just be here as an act. It's got to be real. Let's really deal with some of the real issues." And that just turned that mom around. It just, for some reason, made a real impact on her, and I think it really impacted what she was getting out of the program, also.

And the other thing I told her was—because she was real

concerned, she doesn't have custody of her child — I said, "Go talk to your worker. Be honest. Ask her what your rights are. Who does really have custody? What's it going to take? You know, find out. There's no reason that that could hurt you. In fact, if you're honest with your worker, and that person knows that you're working to your fullest to fulfill what's in your service agreement, then it's to your advantage." And she did that, and I think she really got a lot of information that was helpful, and realized that she likes her worker, and it's not as bad as she had imagined. So, I think there's a lot of difference between what one imagines the agency to do, and what they really do.

CPS was frequently referred to by parents as an entity that superseded the individuals who represented it. Georgia shared a story about a time, early in her career, when she visited a housing project and overheard a warning message being conveyed in loud whispers from neighbor to neighbor as she climbed out of her car, "It's the Welfare." Her story illustrates the notion of individuals within an organization or system being seen as the system itself.

Jean, who generally had good things to say about the individuals and interventions associated with CPS, particularly disliked visiting her children at the CPS office because of the supervision provided by CPS staff. In that situation, Jean saw the people who worked at CPS as the long arms of the agency.

I hated them. They were the world's worst thing. I feel in Russia you would have a bigger and better chance of visiting your kids than in the CPS office. In Russia. It's just the same thing. The only thing that's different is your bodyguard is not armed. That's the only difference. They're right there watching everything you say, watching everything you do. I've learned how to cope with that. I just shut them off, because I know nothing I'm doing or saying is wrong. But at first I really felt intimidated. We were the victims, but yet we were the criminals too.

Along with impressions of being under CPS staff surveillance and feeling fear of punishment if they failed to meet CPS expectations, parents felt humiliated by having their parenting publicly judged. Ann remembered a time shortly after Ben was first removed from home by CPS when she visited him in a small, colorless cubicle at the CPS office. The 1-hour, weekly visits were loaded with emotion which influenced the behavior of both Ben and Ann, and all of it occurred in view of

CPS personnel who observed visits to make certain that parents did not harm their children. Those observations were among Ann's most salient memories of visits with Ben.

> *Susan*: Where were your visits?
> *Ann*: At the office.
> *Susan*: At CPS?
> *Ann*: Yes. And I even got reprimanded — I'll never forget that as long as I live — right there at the office. He's playing with the blinds. You know how you redirect them and all that? And he wouldn't redirect, so I slapped him, slapped his hands. Then that didn't work, so I spanked him. She took him and just read me the riot act, "We don't spank our children here." It was like, "What would you like me to do, lady? Let him rip the blinds off the window? Then I'll get in trouble for that." And I just told her, "Look. When I was raised, you get told something, you better do it or you get spanked." "Well, we don't do that now and da-da-da." It just really upset me. And I asked her, "So does this mean I'm abusing my child?" Then she got on the defensive, and told me not to get smart.

Perhaps the most disturbing interactions were those in which the parents' mental health was questioned by caseworkers. I observed caseworkers relate concerns to parents in a manner that seemed insensitive at best, and even unethical, as this description of a meeting between a parent named Maria and her caseworker makes evident. Maria was a mother in her early twenties whose 2- and 4-year-old children had been in a foster care placement for about a year. I had observed Maria with her children during intervention sessions and interviewed her outside of the Parenting Program. Maria invited me to accompany her to CPS for a meeting with her caseworker and attorney. I phoned Maria's caseworker to ask her permission to attend the meeting. She readily agreed.

As Maria, her 4-year-old son Doug, her caseworker, and I walked from the CPS lobby through a secured door to the meeting room, we passed through a cavernous office area that felt crowded and close despite its size. The room contained what seemed to be close to 100 desks situated a few feet apart in opposing directions. The building was under construction, and wires and exposed pipes hung from the ceiling reminding me of stalactites and stalagmites in a cave. The caseworkers carried on their business as usual.

Earlier that day I had observed four children in the same room who had been brought into custody by police following the bust of a methamphetamine lab in their home. An infant and toddler peered from a playpen situated in a small area surrounded by four desks while their two older siblings played in the remaining cramped space a few feet away. CPS staff attempted to conduct business and supervise the children at the same time.

We entered a small, windowless box with an acoustical ceiling, barren walls, and single desk surrounded by four aluminum frame chairs with orange plastic seats. This was the meeting room. The caseworker explained that Maria's attorney would not attend the meeting, but offered no reason for his absence, and in my field notes I questioned why the attorney, who represented Maria, spoke with Maria's caseworker rather than communicating directly with her. I knew Maria had a phone and could have been reached. Maria did not appear to question his absence or the incongruity of her attorney communicating with CPS rather than her.

The caseworker sat, placed her papers on the desk in front of her, and mentioned that she had a copy of Maria's psychological report. She told Maria to have a seat, motioned to a chair nearest the desk, and turned to face her. Maria sat stiffly, hands folded in her lap, both feet on the floor, and the caseworker handed the 17-page, single-spaced psychological report to her, telling her she could read it later. She reminded Maria that the psychologist had been selected by Maria's attorney, then spoke of "concerns."

The caseworker prefaced her interpretation of the psychological report by telling Maria, "You hated me forever, but that's okay." Maria tensed and turned slightly as if to protest, but sat silently in response to the caseworker's remark. The caseworker, referring to the psychologist by her first name, explained that the test used to evaluate Maria was the MMPI (Minnesota Multiphasic Personality Inventory, a psychological test designed to assess personality traits). As power saws and sledge hammers operated on the opposite side of a wall about 10′ from us, she explained that the report indicated that Maria had "poor judgment regarding her children and their needs," and she made vague reference to a "personality disorder." Maria suggested the label was due to a hospitalization during her adolescent years, and the caseworker questioned whether the hospitalization was because of Maria's drug use, which Maria confirmed.

Maria seemed uncomfortable and offered in advance of hearing the test results that she had seen the psychologist for "only an hour or so" and thought the test was not valid and the answers on the test inadequate, that they were only half-true and did not accurately fit the way she would have responded if she could have explained what she meant. The caseworker countered by saying the test was well-established and some items were included to let the psychologist know if the person taking the test was being honest. She did not mention that the psychologist commented in the report (which Maria later shared with me) that Maria appeared to be giving honest responses during the evaluation. In my field notes, I questioned the caseworker's qualifications to interpret the MMPI. According to Anastasi (1976), the MMPI "is essentially a clinical instrument whose proper interpretation calls for considerable psychological sophistication" (p. 504). I wondered why the psychologist who had administered the test communicated the sensitive results to the caseworker rather than to Maria.

The caseworker abruptly changed from what I suspect was an emotionally upsetting topic for Maria to a review of what Maria needed to do to have her children returned: arrange homemaker visits, enroll her children in the community program, and attend the Parenting Program. She smiled at Maria as she told her, "You won't have to see me but once every 6 weeks." She summarized the meeting, sandwiching requirements and expectations between compliments on Maria's intelligence and criticisms of her parenting. Using an example from the psychologist's report about Maria's use of only verbal explanations to discipline her children, the caseworker raised the issue of Maria's "unreasonable expectations" of her children. Maria explained that the children began using words at 5 and 6 months, walked at 8 months and were "very smart." The caseworker disputed Maria's perceptions with a mention of concerns about "Doug's delays." Doug stopped playing and listened when he heard his name, and Maria flinched. I suspected, and Maria later confirmed, that it was the first time Maria had received any information about her son having developmental problems. The caseworker seemed to notice neither the child's presence nor Maria's reaction as she proceeded through her agenda.

The caseworker handed the psychological report to Maria as we prepared to leave telling her to "read it nondefensively." Maria responded, "If I can. It's about me," then commented that her parents were always telling her she was insane. Maria defended herself by explaining that she just has depression, and the caseworker reassured Maria that she was not insane.

The observation left me feeling uneasy on a number of counts. Because of my professional training in the field of special education and my personal experience of having a brother with autism, I felt great empathy with Maria for having learned about her child's developmental delays. I wondered about the caseworker's expertise in the area of child development and how she had come to know this information about the child. I was certain she had little training in delivering sensitive information to parents; the brevity of her explanation to Maria seemed to reflect her ignorance about the child's diagnosis. It was even more painful to observe Maria as she received diagnostic information about her own mental health in a manner that I could only describe as blunt.

Pauline described a similar situation in which a CPS caseworker commented that she had a "passive aggressive" personality. The caseworker instructed a class that Pauline enrolled in to fulfill part of her service contract with CPS. The class on the foundations of abuse was one Pauline thought helped her to understand the influence of her past on the way she parented Cody. In this interview, I questioned Pauline's understanding of the psychological descriptors applied to her by the caseworker and psychologist.

> *Pauline*: She said that I was passive aggressive. And I even had a psychological test or evaluation, and they said the same thing. It was because of the way I was treated, so I could understand where it was coming from.
>
> *Susan*: Do you understand what she meant by passive aggressive?
>
> *Pauline*: Well, kind of. Not really. Because what happened one time, when we were in class there at the church upstairs, this guy just came waltzing right in, right off the street. Said he was from Seattle or something or other. He didn't say what he was looking for, and he just all the sudden blurted out, "You want to kill me, don't you?" And she watched, and she sat there, and she watched everybody's reaction and everything. And I just told him exactly how it was. "We're having a group right now. You're interrupting our group. We'd like for you to leave, so we can get along with our group. No one wants to kill you. You're the one who interrupted our group." And then she told me that in the right circumstances, I would have gotten hit. And I said, "No, I just plain told him."
>
> I don't know. I really didn't understand it, so I just kind of — and I didn't want to start an argument — I just kind of let it fly over my shoulders. It was quite weird, especially that guy just walking right into class. That really freaked me out, because the kids were in the next room. The first thing I did, before I even said anything to him was got up, went over, let the

babysitter know that there was somebody out here, a transient out here, and that to keep her eye on all them kids and to not let them out of the room.

Susan: That happens in that church a lot. Tell me about the "psychological." You said you had a "psychological" done on you. Was that through CPS?

Pauline: Yeah. They said that I had a high potential for drug and alcohol abuse. They said I was passive aggressive, I was manipulative, and I was also naive. Now, if you're manipulative, how do you put manipulative and naive together?

Susan: I don't know. What do you think about it?

Pauline: I think it was a bunch of bull. You sit here and you answer 569 true-false questions, answering yes or no on stupid stuff like "Do you think people are out to get you?" and all this. Then putting these little blocks together, making a drawing, and putting these blocks together certain ways. How do you come up with how people are, I mean, like that? How do you come up with an evaluation of "you're naive" by how you put these blocks together?

Susan: What did they tell you about it?

Pauline: They didn't tell me nothing about it. I talked to the psychologist myself. He told me, "I think you're perfectly capable of taking care of your kid." But yet he puts in this report that I am manipulative in relationships, and that I'm naive and passive aggressive, and I have a high potential for drug and alcohol abuse. And I have never had a problem like that.

Communication with caseworkers was cautious on the part of parents as evidenced in Pauline's description of a conversation with her caseworker that occurred prior to Cody's return home. The caseworker questioned her motives for wanting Cody returned. Pauline, although upset by her caseworker's accusation, rationalized that it was for the good of her child.

My caseworker said, "Pauline, isn't it true that the only reason why you want your kid back is so you could have welfare, so you don't have to go out and work and earn a living like everybody else around here?" I came this close to slapping her. Of course I thought about it. I could slap her, and then I could get arrested for assault. And they do that. They ask you these questions so they can upset you to see what your reactions are. Which in a way is good because they want to see if you're going to react to your kid that way, but I know a lot of people who react that way to other people but not to a kid. The kids, they don't have any problem with the kids. Then I see other people who don't have their kids back yet because of the way they fly off at CPS. I don't think that I will ever, ever forget what I've gone through.

The caseworker's perceptions of Pauline were contrary to her demonstrated work history and contrary to my experience with her. Her fear and anger seemed justified, but it seemed clear that there was no safe forum in which they could be voiced. The consequences of retaliation were too severe.

The staff expressed frustration about CPS caseworkers' perceptions not only about parents, but also about the Parenting Program. During one post-intervention meeting, one of the family interventionists told her co-workers about a conversation she had with a CPS caseworker. The interventionist had accompanied the caseworker on a home visit with a mother who had recently moved from a motel room to a small rented house in order to have a place for her children when they were returned from foster care. In the parent's eyes, the two-bedroom house with hardwood floors and a view of a nearby river was an improvement over the motel, and she and her boyfriend could live there rent-free for several months while they worked to repair it. The interventionist from the Parenting Program described the house as being in very poor condition with barbed wire and automobile parts strewn about the yard, and a vicious dog tied next door, but she tried to imagine the excitement the mother must have felt leaving the cheap, single room at the motel that had been her home. One staff member asked if the children's safety was an issue because of the close proximity of the house to the river, and the family interventionist answered in a voice resonating with black humor and defeat, no, they would not be in jeopardy from the water, they would probably be injured from a number of other hazards before they ever reached the river.

Although the interventionist from the Parenting Program seemed to agree with the CPS caseworker regarding the questionable safety of the children if they lived in the house, after hearing the caseworker describe the house as looking like a "utilities shack or a chicken coop — exactly like the kind of place you'd run a meth lab" (a laboratory where illegal drugs are manufactured) — and dismiss the family because they were "frustrating," the Parenting Program interventionist felt "down."

I think [the caseworker] feels that we have blinders on. She thinks that parents who are dysfunctional get confused because they're getting positive feedback, and parents who are dysfunctional are not well served by this program because the program is so positive. But how would she know? She's never been to the program . . . If I say something negative, she jots it down right away, but she doesn't seem to believe when I say something nice.

Program co-directors Georgia and Isabelle also related tales of frustration about caseworkers' perceptions of parents. Georgia said their attitudes toward parents' information was "take it with a grain of salt," and that caseworkers always thought parents were hiding something or trying to fool them. Georgia "would be furious if no one believed [her] when [she] said something," and, in fact, she too appeared to meet some skepticism by caseworkers. She described a home visit in which she had conducted an assessment of the physical environment and parent-child interactions. When she reported that "things looked really good," the caseworker responded by rolling her eyes.

Pauline's description of CPS, related over a year after her case was closed, Cody was returned, and she had voluntarily returned to the Parenting Program, was in accord with Georgia's impression that caseworkers were skeptical of parents' honesty.

When the Parenting Program said they wanted to come do a visit, I got scared. I really did. I explained to Cody's teacher what had happened in the past and the reason why it intimidated me. CPS— like I said before, there's really no word to describe them. They're manipulative. Because I can see there's some caseworkers who don't believe in the parents and really don't give the parents a fair try. And I've seen it, and I guess maybe since I've seen it, I should report it. But why? It's not going to go nowhere. Nobody has power over CPS.

Isabelle attributed the miscommunication in part to the caseworkers being "overworked." Large caseloads made the daily demands of case management impossible, thus caseworkers stopped — or appeared to stop — trying to perform their jobs conscientiously. "I have a terrible time ever getting a hold of them. There are certain ones who do always call back and that are more conscientious, it seems. There are others that are very hard to get a hold of, who don't respond, who make judgments without ever observing the program. So I think there are a lot of camps within the agency itself, and that some parents get great services, depending on who the worker is; other parents don't get the services they need at all." Isabelle shared her views about the previously described home visit that was conducted by the program interventionist and the CPS caseworker.

> There have been a couple of situations here at the Parenting Program where a family hasn't been fulfilling their parent training goals, and maybe doesn't show up. And in one particular instance, the caseworker happened to visit that day, but had never visited before when the parents were there. So the interventionist went out with that caseworker to the home, and it was a pretty terrible situation as far as the kind of home, and it just reconfirmed what the caseworker already thought. On the way back, the caseworker shared with our teacher that this program didn't work, it was a joke, it was too loosey-goosey, it was too relaxed, we don't really follow through with our parents who really don't stick to their goals.
>
> It was very upsetting to the staff. The teacher became very upset from what I heard in our debriefing session, and basically it was upsetting to us because we were saying, if that's their impression of us, then why are we trying to work with all these clients from CPS and help them fulfill their service agreement? Really, they think we're a joke.

The staff of the Parenting Program believed that the intervention techniques they used were perceived by caseworkers to be inadequate in treating families. But those very techniques had only recently come to be valued by interventionists in the Parenting Program. One of the program staff commented about how the program had changed over time, and one of the most important changes, she believed, was in the attitudes of staff members toward parents as well as in the previously held belief that staff needed little training to provide intervention to families. She recalled that when she first worked in the program, she thought that "anybody could do this." But now she believed that there was a growing recognition among program staff that certain skills were needed by interventionists "in order to really have success with the parents."

> Things like empathy, and communication skills — how you portray yourself to a family or how you're coming off to a family — I think those are really important for success. I think we used to be desperate for somebody to come in and work with a family, and now, we've stepped back and looked, and said, "Gee, do you think that person is ready?" or "I think they need to observe another time,"

or "This person looks like they would be really good with parents, they seem to have those kinds of skills already."

The curriculum and strategies employed at the program evolved over time, and although the program experienced staff turnover, a strong core of staff members remained to promote consistency and continuity of the program's philosophy and goals. The philosophy, intervention strategies, and goals were clearly related in theory and practice in the program and were easily recognizable to families. Although caseworkers may have thought Parenting Program staff were ineffectual and too gentle, the parents did not agree. The qualities they valued, wanted, and sometimes received included access to knowledge and skills to help them parent, access to services that could help their families to survive, and people who would treat them with dignity while helping them to acquire those things they wanted and needed.

SUPPORTING FAMILIES BY EMPOWERING PARENTS

Pauline identified compassion among staff members as an important attribute of the program: "I've also seen the caring that's there, that they really do care about what's happening, and you're not just a somebody who's going through." Ann talked about wanting to "get a bottle and forget her problems" when Ben was in intensive care in the hospital for an asthma attack. Instead, she told me, "I went to the program because I wanted to drink really bad, and I thought, they won't mind if you come down here. So, I came down here."

What made the program welcoming to parents despite their participation having resulted from involvement with CPS? Perhaps the answer lies in the program's philosophy as it was described by one of the interventionists.

> *Susan*: How would you describe the philosophy of the program?
> *Program Interventionist*: The basic philosophy would be keeping families together, or reuniting families in a healthy environment, [which means] parent education, sort of reparent education, for a lot of families who are relearning parenting skills or learning new parenting skills.
> *Susan*: Other people have used that word "reparent." Tell me more about what that means.
> *Program Interventionist*: Well, you always hear that you learn how to parent from your own parents, and . . . I can really see

how that's true after working with these families because they really did learn how to parent from their parents. Reparenting is giving them new options for parenting, learning how to be a different kind of parent than their parents were often times—options that don't necessarily have to include different forms of abuse—be it emotional or physical—or neglect. I guess that's what reparenting is. In a way, sometimes I think we parent our parents too, a little bit, in terms of helping them build their own self-esteem and that sort of thing.

Susan: Tell me more about that.

Program Interventionist: I think that self-esteem is an issue for a lot of our parents, although they may not recognize it as such. A lot of them will respond in different ways. Either they'll be very angry, or very—I don't want to say complacent—but they'll be eager to please, but not necessarily feel the concept of what it is we're trying to put across to them. So, I think a lot of it is that they're intimidated by the fact that we're coming on as the professionals, and they've always been intimidated by professionals. I think that has a lot to do with their image of themselves. Self-esteem is an issue that we deal with a lot.

Susan: What do you do about that? What can you do?

Program Interventionist: Primarily, it seems like I spend a lot of time reassuring people that I'm not there to make judgments necessarily about them, but what I want from them is to have a happy household where people are getting along, or at least they have options for dealing with anger or frustration or whatever, and preventing the kinds of power struggles and blow ups that happen in families where there aren't those options. You reassure them by letting them know that you know that is what they really want too because I think it is what they really want. They may not be able to express it. But once they start hearing about options, it's as if they'd like that, but they're resistant to it because they don't think that it will work.

It's convincing someone. You reassure people, praise parents the same way you would do in a classroom [of children]. You let someone know what it is you like about what they're doing, or what you think is going to work for them, building on the positive things that are going on, rather than pointing to all the faults that are happening. And I think you can address those issues, and that doesn't have to be negative either.

Susan: How can you keep it from being negative?

Program Interventionist: I think by letting the parents know that you feel that they can accomplish those options, that it isn't out of the question for them.

Nearly half of the parents in the program were raised by families who had also been involved with CPS. The impact of having been poorly parented that was so evident in the parents' childhood histories, combined with their youth when they became parents, was evidenced in their interactions with their children and with others. Some played with toys rather than with their children in the classroom, and the children's needs for food, clothes, and nurturing were often subjugated to the parents' needs. The influence of their own childhoods was perhaps most apparent in the parents' sense of and perceptions about themselves. Pauline, Ann, and Jean related changes in their feelings of self-esteem, and they attributed those changes in part to the Parenting Program. Jean expressed the belief that her feelings of self-worth stemmed from her newly learned parenting skills.

A year-and-a-half ago, I wouldn't even have called it a family there was so much anger and stuff. I didn't take care of the kids. I didn't do nothing for the kids. And now, since I've taken parenting classes, I understand the kids. I take care of the kids. I know what to do. I know why they're crying, or why they're being fussy. It's not because they want to be, it's because something's wrong. And before I never understood that. It's helped a great deal. My family — it's really changed. It's nice too. It's almost unreal. . . .

Before I didn't care if my house was clean. I didn't care if my kids were clean. I didn't care if they breathed much less anything else. And now I stay home. I take care of my children. I make sure they have clean clothes. I make sure that they have the things they need.

Overall I'm a better person. I'm a better parent by far, but I think it comes with self-approval. Because I had a really low self-esteem, and now I'm proud of myself. I've accomplished a lot. The kids see it too.

As I mentioned previously, Jean's testimonials are always somewhat suspect, but I also entertain the possibility that Jean actually saw herself and the situation greatly improved, and it may have been.

Pauline attributed changes in her situation in part to the Parenting Program, but she also spoke of the support and parenting she received from outside the Parenting Program. When she first became involved with CPS, Pauline received help from a couple who, she believed, were her salvation.

After Pauline and Cody had been placed in separate foster homes by CPS, Pauline ran from the foster care home to a couple who, although they were not biologically related to Pauline, had "always been friends . . . like grandparents." The couple had encouraged Pauline to "get squared away with CPS and get Cody back." Their support of Pauline was apparent in their application to become certified foster parents so that Pauline could reside with them while she worked to regain custody.

The couple received $319 per month from CPS during the year Pauline stayed with them, and they spent $150 of it on Pauline's schooling. They also gave her $44 for clothing and $46 for personal items each month—money she budgeted carefully so that it would last the month.

Pauline's schedule during that time began at 6:30 a.m. when she arose to get ready for school. It was a difficult schedule because she worked four, 10½ hour shifts at a mill 4 days a week and did not get to sleep until 3:00 a.m. on those days. One day a week she attended the Parenting Program where she visited Cody, and one day a week she attended church with her "grandparents." With the support of the couple, Pauline completed school that year—"went through graduation and everything."

Pauline attributed her success in completing school and regaining custody of Cody to her friends. They were, she said, "superb grandparents. . . . They made me go back to school. They made me do UAs [urine assays]. They made me get my own place, on my own." A transition of power from CPS to the couple and eventually to Pauline occurred. Pauline was supported through the transition by two people who wanted to see her succeed and believed she could.

Georgia wanted to name the program PEP—for Parenting Empowerment Program, but her co-workers thought empowerment "sounded too militant." She also considered calling the program the "Parenting Enrichment Program," but thought that empowerment more accurately reflected what she wanted to say.

> I want to empower them and want them to feel a sense of control over their own lives. I think that whenever they become angry and abusive, a lot of it is feeling a lack of control, a lack of power in their lives.

Georgia struggled with her colleagues' criticism about her interactions with families, and frequently subjected herself to examination during our conversations.

Georgia: You know, maybe I have rose-colored glasses, but I try and look for anything that will confirm — no, I'm objective. I've got to admit. I wrote a report recently that didn't say anything positive except that the mother came well-groomed. That was a hard one to write. So, I can't lie. I think I am pretty objective. I try to be objective. But, by God, I also really look for all those good positive things. In fact, I was talking to the caseworker the other day about how difficult it was to tell this parent some relatively negative feedback because I'd said so many positive things that they might think that I'd been lying all that time, like, "Georgia you always said they were doing so well and now you're telling us this." And this caseworker overheard me and she said, "Well, that's your problem. Your problem is, you can't teach those people by praising them." And I said, "Well, I think that is the only way you teach them. It's not the only way, but we've got to reinforce the things they're doing." She said, "They don't learn that way. These people do not learn that way. You've got to point it out to them. You've got to point out their little faults, otherwise they'll think that they're doing okay."

Susan: What do you think about that?

Georgia: You've got to identify areas of need, areas of concern, that has to happen, but there are ways of doing [it] that make parents feel decent about themselves. And, also, you've got to strengthen the things that they're doing that are right already. I know that I'd feel terrible about myself if all I heard were negative things that I was doing wrong. I think you have to have a balance that is heavily weighted on the things you're doing right for you to feel good enough about yourself to deal with the things you're doing wrong. Otherwise, I'd give up.

A lot of our parents have very fragile lives. They've been downtrodden and stomped on so long, they probably already feel like giving up. And, I want to pep them up. I want to empower them a little bit. So, I really work hard at focusing on the things that they're doing right.

Parents did feel a sense of empowerment after participating in the program. After Ann described feelings of increased competence in parenting Ben during parent-child labs, I asked her if she was different in other parts of her life. She responded, "I'm trying to be. I'm trying to stand up for myself and stand by what I believe instead of if somebody says something, I do it, then I regret it because I should have listened to my gut feelings. I'm trying to stand by my convictions and listen to what my gut says instead of listening to other people."

Isabelle commented that the program didn't work "unless people became motivated at some point in the training" to change; she did not "believe you can force it on people if it's really going to work. You can force it on people, you can make people come, but it's really not going to work unless they learn something and unless they can take it and go home and use it." Isabelle was willing to wait for parents' readiness to learn, but expressed dismay about the 21 families that had been involved with CPS for over 6 months before they came to the program and was frustrated with a "bureaucracy" that allowed the program to serve only those people who were in the CPS system—those who had already failed.

COMING FULL CIRCLE: PREVENTING MALTREATMENT

Parenting is a challenging job for all parents—even those with adequate resources. But the extraordinary demands of parenting children with health problems, such as the prematurity and respiratory and cardiac disease experienced by Cody, the colic, impetigo, asthma, and ear infections experienced by Ben, or the prematurity and apnea experienced by several of Jean's children, were compounded by the parents' youth, inexperience in parenting, poverty, and absence of supportive friends and family. Although any of these issues may be predictive of poor developmental outcomes or family crises, none was addressed adequately in Pauline's, Ann's, or Jean's lives prior to the time they had been identified as abusive parents by Child Protective Services and became involved with the Parenting Program.

In order to obtain services from CPS, a negative outcome must already have occurred; parents must have already been identified as failing to provide adequate care to their children. The system operates based on a model of tertiary prevention and responds only after parents are seen as wrong, deviant, guilty, or inadequate. Treatment is made available to parents only after their behavior is identified as criminal by a legal system that operates in partnership—and at cross purpose—with a child welfare system whose stated mission is to preserve families and protect the safety and welfare of children. Legal intervention is available at the outset, but parents and children wait for therapeutic intervention aimed at family preservation or child welfare, if they ever receive it at all. Twenty-one families had been involved with Child

Protective Services for more than 6 months before they eventually received family intervention from the Parenting Program.

Pauline described aspects of the Parenting Program that she liked and the ways in which it helped her to become a better parent, but added, "The one thing I kind of feel bad for is that to get in the Parenting Program, you have to be involved with CPS, or past involved, which is hard because there are so many other parents out there that need the help desperately, and are in such desperate need and can't get what people at CPS can. Even if I didn't have to be involved with CPS I know there are numerous places where I can take Cody, but I wouldn't because of what the Parenting Program is."

Although parents valued the Parenting Program, staff regretted that intervention was available to families only after their problems were obvious enough to attract the attention of CPS. Isabelle expressed frustration that the program couldn't "provide services for our families who aren't in the system yet, who need it, who want it, but because of limited funds, because of limited people, because of limited space, because of the way the grant's written, we can't provide that." During an interview, I asked Isabelle about the ways parents came to the program.

> *Susan*: You said that most parents come to you from CPS, but some of them come to you because they are at risk for abusing their children.
> *Isabelle*: They just feel stressed out. They're afraid of what they're going to do with their child. I had a dad call me up in tears because he just didn't know what to do anymore. He used every technique. He didn't have any technique. He was frustrated; he was crying on the phone. So [with] that particular parent, I went right out and did a home visit and got him involved in the community therapeutic preschool program and referred him to the Parenting Program. He didn't go into the Parenting Program, but that doesn't mean he won't. I think he wasn't ready at the time because he was dealing with some other issues. We also have some parents in our community program who we might target as needing some help.
> *Susan*: So they might not even be in CPS?
> *Isabelle*: Right. We have the option to take some people from the Community Program, and I think we even took a family recently, and I've been talking with them. Someone who really wanted help but didn't have an open CPS case, and [who] Georgia kind of took her under her wing, started going to didactic

parent training programs at night, but she really wanted to come to something where she could be with her children and get feedback when she's interacting with her children. So we found a way to fit her in. I had three requests this month for the Parenting Program from people in the community, but as we're set up now, we really can't provide that. . . . We take a high percentage of children from CPS, and a small percentage of people from the Community Program.

One of the program staff explained that families were referred primarily by CPS because their children were in or were recently returned from foster care placements. She concurred with Isabelle about the late onset of intervention and suggested an alternative approach, a less intense version of the program she jokingly called "Parenting Program Light." In the "light" version, she explained, parents could voluntarily seek assistance. An added advantage would be that the staff wouldn't have "to tiptoe around the issue of CPS."

Some families sought assistance from the Parenting Program voluntarily, but as Isabelle said, resources weren't available to serve all who would have liked to attend. Georgia estimated that she received an average of two phone calls each week from parents not involved with CPS but who recognized that they needed help learning to parent. Most heard about the program from parents who had participated and felt successful after having attended the program. Georgia always tried to find other services in the community for families she couldn't serve, but services were scarce and not always appropriate for the families' needs. Occasionally she heard from them again, but only after their lives deteriorated to the point of CPS involvement and court-mandated parent training.

"THESE KIDS DO NOT COME WITH PARENTING MANUALS"

Acquiring the knowledge and skills to provide care for and strengthen relationships with their children were among the most important outcomes of attending the Parenting Program mentioned by parents. Although an awareness (or admission) that one's parenting was substandard was often a consequence of families' involvement with CPS, ideas of what constituted ideal parenting were not easily grasped — especially by parents who had been raised in homes that operated according to standards that were very different from those of CPS.

When Jean, at age 14, brought her newborn daughter home from the hospital to her sister's house, she did not have a clue how to go about parenting her child: "What do you do with a baby who screams at 3:00 in the morning, and you don't know what's wrong, and it won't take it's bottle, won't burp?" In Jean's case, her sister assumed care of the baby, and Jean "came and went as [she] pleased" until she became pregnant and gave birth to a second daughter. Two infants were too much for Jean's family, so she was out on her own and "didn't know what in the hell [she] was doing." Jean described the situation her young daughters faced with their young mother:

> I was 16 at the time, lived in my own apartment, and I seriously did not know what to do. I thought, the way Mom handled it was she ignored us, so that's what I should do. And I ignored the kids. [My infant daughter] laid in the bedroom from the moment she woke up until the time she went to bed, and she was still in the room. I'd go in to change her and give her a bottle and feed her, and that was it. She laid in there. And [my toddler] did her own little thing out in the front room. She wasn't getting into nothing so she could be out in the front room. She wasn't aggravating.

Jean's statement, "These kids do not come with parenting manuals," revealed an awareness that the care she provided her children was not adequate, and, moreover, that she did not know how to go about providing adequate care for her children. This recognition among parents about their lack of parenting skills seemed to accompany their acquisition of more successful parenting techniques, as Pauline's observations suggest.

> There was so much that I didn't know that I thought I knew — which in the end, I really did get to know, because they taught me. They don't hover over you. If you are making mistakes, they don't say, "Look, you're doing this wrong, You can't do that. That's not acceptable." They say, "Well, we see this happening, and a suggestion is, and this is how to help, and this may be of some help."

Pauline's example illustrates a central theme of this study: being labeled a "bad parent" doesn't help one become a "good parent." As one parent told me, her eyes full of tears, she didn't need to hear from the caseworker that it was her own fault that she did not have her children. She knew that and "had to live with it everyday."

Isabelle believed parents "learn to be parents, they aren't born to be parents." She described the needs of parents enrolled in the program in a way consistent with both developmental and ecological models of intervention. "Many of us operate as parents at lots of different development levels based on the way that we were parented, based on our age when we have children, based on our educational background." She described parents in the program as "very high need" and having "minimal parenting skills," but said that "within the group there are developmental levels of functioning, too." Isabelle's description of the intervention approach employed in the Parenting Program illustrates how the program staff attempted to individualize intervention for families according to their needs and interests.

> There are some parents who have the idea that they don't want to hit their children to discipline them, and they really want to find out how to be a better parent, how to get more structure into their lives and into their homes so that they can build a relationship with their child. There are other parents that come into the program, who really don't think they need it, or they're very afraid and angry, and they're not open to the kind of training that we provide. But they develop a trust over a period of time, most of them, because the program that we offer is really a family-focused kind of program, and it's hands on.
>
> It's process oriented. In other words, we don't sit the parents down in a class and lecture to them about what we, the experts, think they should do to be the perfect parent. We try to look at them as individuals and to look at them developmentally, and to look at what they want to learn as well as what we might have observed in dealing with their children. We see some goals we need to work on, or, also in working with Child Protective Services there may be some specific goals that they need to work on to get their kids back. So, the reason I think our program works as well as it does—and I don't think it's successful for every parent—is because we invite the parents with their children into a play lab where it's fun. There are activities set up that they can participate in and [they can] play with their kids. They learn that play is really important, and they almost get permission to play. Maybe they never got to play when they were kids. It's something maybe they're experiencing for the first time, or at least the awareness of the importance of play [is new].
>
> The lab is set up informally so that parents can just be comfortable. We try to sit down so they don't think we're all watching

them, because at first that's really hard to handle. And in the lab, they have a person that works with them on a one-to-one basis and gives them feedback when it's needed or if their child has a tantrum. Somebody might say, "Well, what do you think you should do?" We're giving them a chance to come up with a solution. But, if they don't know, maybe we'd give them a suggestion, or maybe we would talk to them in our (debriefing) meetings on a one-to-one basis: "How did it go today when he had that tantrum at lunch? It seemed like he really got upset about that. Let's talk about what might have worked better than what you did." So, the kind of parent training program that we're offering includes didactic sessions where we go over some specific items such as behavior management and child development to give them some foundation and background. But the lab, where they come with their children, I feel is what makes all the difference. We're not just sitting them at desks. We're actually providing the situations where they can be with their kids and these behaviors and issues can come out in a safe place and they can get immediate help. . . .

Jean was one of those parents who, by her own admission, had great needs. As this interview attests, the program was helpful in addressing some of them.

When they took my kids, they said I have this certain period of time to get my parenting and my mom's group going and get a house. Not only go to my parenting [classes], but improve my parenting. And I thought, okay, whatever. I'll play your game. That's the attitude that I had then. I'd have done anything to get my kids back home. When I went to the parenting [class], it was so very different from what I imagined. It was actually helpful. I thought you had to be a bunch of fuddy-duddies sitting around telling me, "You're doing this wrong, and you're doing this wrong," and it's not like that. It's so helpful.

My interventionist, I just love her. She's always trying to help. She doesn't only tell me what I'm doing wrong, she tells me how to get what I'm doing wrong going right. She gives me pointers how to deal with it. That's what you need. It's not so much knowing what you're doing wrong, it's that she gives me pointers how to correct what I'm doing wrong. That's what people need. I think people should be made to take a parenting class in high school. I think it should be a high school diploma kind of a thing.

I had kids thinking that you had them, and you dress them up all nice and pretty, and then you go out and you show them off, and then you come home and you put them up on this little thing and just go "night baby," and "I don't want to deal with you no more. I've had it. That's enough." It's not like that. God! I woke up real fast.

You know when I had my first baby, I went through my whole pregnancy going, "Yes! I'm going to have a baby. I can go show her off, and dress her up real cute, and go shopping." And I never knew that it required so much time, care, understanding, patience. On and on. There's just so much to having a baby. And I wasn't ready for her. I really wasn't. She had 6 long years of pain for me not being ready to have her. That's why I'd never recommend it to my worst enemy to have babies at 14.

Ann's reflections about the Parenting Program also affirmed Isabelle's interpretation of the approach and illustrated the impact it had not only on her knowledge of and skill in parenting her child, but also on how she viewed her child and their relationship: "I'm starting to learn how to enjoy him and not focus so much on his tyrant behavior, and that's a plus. Because for awhile I was getting so wrapped up in the negative, I didn't even know when he was good. I'm learning how to enjoy him, and when he smiles or does something cute, to treasure that."

Pauline commented on the changes she and Cody experienced since they first became involved with the Parenting Program.

> *Pauline:* I've done a lot of screwing up. Lucky I've done it early in my life so that I can learn and change and work for things.
> *Susan:* Everybody does a little screwing up along the way. How would you say Cody's doing?
> *Pauline:* I've seen a remarkable change in Cody, in his behavior especially. It was the environment. We were just talking about this yesterday in the Parenting Program, about the positive things. And I told [Georgia], now that we've moved he's got more room to play, he's a lot happier. Before he was [on] my nerves constantly, and now I only have to send him to the corner once every 3 or 4 days because he's just turned into a little good boy. And that's what I want, I want Cody to be happy, and I want him to live a happy and successful life.

The acquisition of parenting skills in the context of the Parenting Program was necessary to foster family functioning and to help parents exit the child welfare system, but it was not always sufficient given some of the parents' life circumstances outside the program. One might question the pertinence of focusing primarily on the teaching of discrete parenting skills when other, more pressing issues remained unaddressed. As is evident from earlier stories of Pauline's and other families' lives, and the circumstances that brought them to and kept them involved with CPS, parenting their children during intervention sessions was only one among many challenges. Poverty, homelessness, illness, unhappiness, hopelessness, violence, alcohol, and drugs surrounded parents and children and were difficult to combat, but necessary to confront.

INTERVENTION IN THE CONTEXTS OF FAMILY AND COMMUNITY

The parents revealed their awareness of changes in their lives and a newly discovered sense of control over life after intervention, but changes did not result from a single agency or program; rather, a number of interventions and support received from many sources over a long period of time seemed to contribute to change, as these excerpts from interviews with Ann convey.

> [I used to be] angry and all that. And I choose not to be. I have every right to be angry and bitter at CPS, I think. But I learned a lot in AA too. All during my childhood I walked around angry, and resentful, and bitter, and hateful, and it didn't get me anywhere but drunk and into a lot of trouble. It doesn't do any good. . . .
>
> I've had a lot of therapy, finally, in the last 6 years. I've finally had a lot of therapy to help me, along with AA. So I'm not scared to ask for help anymore. If I need help, I'll go get help somehow, somewhere.
>
> I've always been a victim, [a] helpless victim. Now I don't want to be a victim anymore. People think that you can just make that change, but it's not easy. It's scary, because all my life I've been a victim, and I've let other people do things to me. I've always looked to a man. If he said that I was a good wife, then I was a good wife. If he said I was a good mother, then I was a good mother.

The man Ann looked to for approval was her husband, and her initial involvement with CPS resulted as much from her violent, drunken, volatile relationship with him as from the incident that Sunday morning she shook her infant son because he wouldn't stop crying and drink from his bottle. Her caseworker's acknowledgment that if you're married, "you don't get into these kinds of situations by yourself," and her visits to Ann's home to observe her interactions with Ben, gave Ann a feeling of hope that she could correct her problems with the CPS and the legal system. Her previous caseworker "never gave [her] a chance. Never came to the house. Nothing. She just made up her mind."

The Parenting Program attempted to "work with the whole family as much as possible," according to Isabelle, and although spouses or partners didn't always participate, the staff always worked with parents and children, and "sometimes even the extended family if they've been a support system." Pauline believed the practice of "parents and children attending intervention all together" was a much better method than in the previous classes she attended at CPS where "the kids weren't brought up a lot."

Aside from building relationships within families, parent-child intervention helped to address the universal problem of child care—a major barrier to participation in CPS classes, counseling, and meetings. For Jean, who had "something with CPS everyday," coming to the program with her children was a relief. But child care was necessary if parents were to obtain other services. Ann commented that she had no child care for AA meetings, and jokingly told me that if she brought Ben with her to the meetings, everyone would need to go out for a drink afterward.

In addition to parent-child labs and home visits, information about and referrals to other needed services were provided by the program along with efforts to help families find ways to access and pay for those services. Georgia enumerated, "respite care, free clothes, free food, cheap counseling, a phone number of a friend—some sort of support, even if it's just one other person that they feel comfortable in phoning," among families' needs. Another Parenting Program interventionist explained the need to identify circumstances that precipitated problems rather than focusing on immediate problems outside the contexts in which they occurred. When I asked her what kinds of things families needed from the program she provided examples.

Here's a family that's stressed out because there's no income, or a mom [who's] stressed out because she's depressed and frustrated because she doesn't think she has a future, or she needs some time to get away from her children. [Parents need] the basic kinds of things: child care, housing, counseling is a big one, drug and alcohol treatment, those kinds of things. The kinds of things that there isn't any money for."

The greatest barrier to obtaining needed help was inadequate finances — without exception, this was an issue for families trying to regain custody of their children. One mother, who has mild mental retardation, acknowledged needing counseling to deal with the sexual abuse by her brothers and father that she had suffered as a child. She had attended 13 counseling sessions at a cost of $10 each — an enormous sum to her — and while she tried to attend the sessions every week, she canceled appointments when she did not have money to pay for them. The mother reported that her attorney reminded her that she must attend the sessions in order to regain custody of her children and that her children were more important than money. Although she agreed that her children were more important than money, she believed that she "shouldn't have to choose."

Families enrolled in the Parenting Program related that they had received nurturing and support from the staff, and that they had acquired knowledge and skills that bolstered their feelings of self-worth and fostered a sense of control over their lives. By accounts from the parents and staff members, the parents' abilities to provide adequate care for their children improved when compared to their initial involvement with CPS. However, questions remained regarding the adequacy of those skills, and even when they were adequate, whether families could maintain them over time and outside the supportive structure of the program.

CHAPTER 6

GETTING OUT OF THE SYSTEM

In the first place, their clients are afraid of them. They're intimidated . . . I think the worse part of it is the mental anguish that people go through with CPS. I think that is about the worst because you feel like there's no way to end. I remember when I first started in with CPS, I didn't think I would ever get my child back.
—Pauline

Regardless of whether parents were eventually successful in regaining custody of their children, involvement with CPS usually was protracted. Twenty-two of the 55 parents had been involved with CPS longer than 6 months prior to their enrollment in the Parenting Program. Once enrolled, however, most successfully completed the program. Only three parents who enrolled during the first year of this study failed to complete at least one 14-week session. Ten families completed a single 14-week session, and 33 families enrolled in the Parenting Program attended two or three 14-week sessions. Most families also regained custody of their children after completing the program.

Although 50 of the 55 parents had children who were under CPS jurisdiction at the time they entered the Parenting Program, and two-thirds were in substitute care, 45 of the parents had reestablished custody of their children by the time they finished the program. Of the 45 parents who regained custody of their children, 39 parents retained custody of their children 6 months after they completed the Parenting Program. How did CPS determine whether parents could or would provide safe environments for their children once they were returned to them? Georgia offered her impression of the basis on which CPS decided when children should be returned to their parents.

How do parents get out of the CPS system and resume their lives? I think it's guess work. They're in this program. They have the opportunity to demonstrate [their ability to parent] while they're here with the children. We can record whether they can, in a controlled setting, adequately care for their children. Until the children are returned home, or have extended home visits, we can't assess whether they can maintain the skills and generalize them to the home environment. There is always a risk. There is no assessment out there, there is no way of knowing or predicting how children are going to do once they are returned to the home.

If they're not in the parent training program, they have visits at the CPS office in the small rooms for an hour a week, and the caseworker sees whether or not parents attend and sees whether or not they go to their counseling appointments or their drug treatment appointments. That's basically it. Do they do what they're told to do? The compliant parents are the ones who get the results, regardless of what they can demonstrate with their children.

Program co-director Isabelle expressed similar concerns about a mother referred to the program for intervention whose parental rights were terminated prior to completion of her first 14-week session. According to Isabelle, the caseworker never observed the parent in the program and talked to Isabelle briefly over the phone only once about the mother's performance during intervention sessions. Although the parent had attended every session, was responsive to feedback from staff, had received positive reports from her interventionist, and had a temporary job and was looking for permanent work, the caseworker had reservations about the mother. Isabelle thought the caseworker was concerned about the length of time the parent was taking to find permanent employment and housing. Isabelle believed that caseworkers did not consider all available evidence when they made decisions to pursue termination of parental rights:

I really had hope for this parent. I saw a lot of other [parents] who were a lot worse. Again, there's a discrepancy between some people getting 3 years of chances, which I don't agree with either. I think that there has to be some kind of decision made for the child's sake — and others getting the absolute minimum. And is that based on agency standards, or is that based on a law, or is that based on just the caseworker's whim? Sometimes I feel a lot of decisions are made based on the caseworker's whim, and that concerns me.

Most families did complete the program without their parental rights being legally terminated, and the program began to make multiple 14-week sessions available to parents who wanted or needed intervention longer than 14 weeks. One of the program staff called this "return business" and thought it was great. After all, she asked, "What more positive thing could you say about a program than that a parent sees it as helpful?" The 10 parents of the 55 enrolled in the program who stayed a year or longer were another matter, however. When weeks stretched into months or years, the program staff became discouraged with parents' lack of progress. Some parents did not acquire the skills necessary to exit the program, although they successfully completed CPS service contracts. This situation forced decisive action from CPS — action not always in the child's best interest. If parents attended the program, completed service contracts, and weren't reported for maltreatment, their cases were sometimes closed and children returned, despite misgivings from program staff about the well-being of the children.

Jean was a case in point. Explaining why she attended the program for a period of over 2 years, she said "the best visiting time [she] ever had was at the Parenting Program." She neglected to mention that program attendance was required by CPS, and as soon as her children were returned to her and attendance at the program was no longer mandated, the children's appearance and the condition of Jean's home deteriorated. Immediately after her last child was returned to her, she stopped attending the Parenting Program, her youngest children stopped attending the community therapeutic preschool program, and her 8-year-old daughter stopped attending public school. I wondered if Jean was on Isabelle's mind when she talked about families for whom the Parenting Program did not work.

> It's pretend, almost, because they're doing what they know they're supposed to do to get through the program, to get their child back, or to get off the case load at CPS, when in actuality, they're in a lot of pain about other issues in their lives. They learn how to play the game, but they don't necessarily integrate it. And then they stop coming.

The reasons for closing cases could be as ambiguous as the reasons for opening them. Every parent and staff member with whom I spoke believed actual incidents of maltreatment were just one of many reasons families became involved with CPS. Staff members mentioned family instability, parents with mental health problems, parents with mental retardation, lack of money, lack of jobs, and lack of clean, safe (or sometimes any) homes. Welfare payments, sheltered housing, violence, counseling, and waiting lists for alcohol and drug treatment programs, boyfriends in jail, problems with parents, and lack of health care or unpaid medical bills were frequently experienced by the families I observed. Like becoming engaged with CPS, becoming disengaged hinged on more than competent parenting skills.

Intervention offered by CPS appeared to be based on the narrow perspective of a parent harming a child, so intervention focused on "fixing" parents. Sometimes the perspective and intervention broadened to include the parent and child, or in the case of the Parenting Program, families. However, parents needing long-term, intensive, comprehensive support and services waited instead for treatment or received brief didactic classes of questionable value while their children, whose psychological, emotional, and developmental needs were rarely mentioned much less addressed, spent years in sequential foster care placements. Meier and Sloan (1984) noted that parents feel trapped in intervention programs that profess to strengthen parenting skills and reunite families but instead lead to relinquishment of parental rights as the goals of court-related services, child protective services, and therapeutic intervention services operate at cross purposes. A program interventionist suggested a treatment approach she thought would be more helpful than the approaches commonly employed by CPS and more relevant to the situations that precipitated CPS involvement.

> The things that grab your attention are the real shocking things. Those are the types of things people like to hear about, the real sensational stuff. . . . There are really serious kinds of things where it was really appropriate to remove children because they had to be protected, where children were in danger, physical danger, where they had been hurt, seriously hurt or injured, or where there was chronic sexual abuse or neglect to the degree that a child's life was in danger, and they were not being supervised at all. But a lot of times, more often than not, families come to us who have those same issues, but on a much smaller scale. It's more "iffy." There is neglect, but the child hasn't been hurt necessarily, or there is neglect, but it would be easier, in my mind, to step in and, instead of removing the child, bombard them with services.
>
> When families come to us, they are really angry because CPS has taken their child away. That flies in the face of what we're trying to do ourselves, which is be positive, to tell our parents, "We need to think in terms of what your children can do, rather than what they can't do," that kind of thing. Yet, here's the protective service agency coming in and doing the antithesis of that, which is to yank the child out. The parent becomes angry and defensive, then they're harder to deal with, and I don't blame

them. I would be really doubtful of something that somebody was telling me after they had come in and taken my child away from me. I would wonder about their motivation. Obviously, they think, "I'm a terrible parent. I'm not a good enough parent to have my child in my home."

Mismatches between societal problems and the policies designed to address them are common. Policymakers want easy solutions, but at the same time they want them to be comprehensive and lasting. Federal monies to develop promising interventions are given to local programs with the extraordinary expectation that those programs will quickly and cleanly reverse the profound damage sustained by families involved with child welfare. Monies are allocated for limited periods of time, and after federal projects end society's problems remain and communities must find ways to continue offering intervention — intervention that might never have been necessary if the basic resources that families needed in the first place to keep from becoming involved with child welfare were available. Well-intentioned professionals make promises in order to obtain funding and to respond to the urgent needs of children and families, and they begin to believe quick, easy solutions are possible.

Rather than looking for comprehensive solutions, child welfare agencies set standards that aim toward efficient disposition of cases rather than effective and lasting outcomes for families. Those policies and practices perpetuate simplistic notions of parents as "bad" and unreasonable expectations that legal intervention will make child maltreatment disappear. But parents who maltreat children because of abuse in their personal histories, drug or alcohol addictions, lack of competent parenting skills, or poor socioeconomic situations rather than malevolence will not become "good parents" by virtue of an agency simply deeming them "bad parents" and removing their children from their care. The problems that bring families to CPS are complicated, persistent, and deeply rooted in parents' personal histories and in contexts outside intervention settings. As Ann started a second year in the program, she wrote a letter to me expressing her reactions to the poverty and isolation she faced when her husband abruptly abandoned her and their son. She emphasized a phrase that left me with the impression that she didn't know how to go about changing her life: "I'm in this awful rut right now, and *I can't seem to do the things I need to do to make it better.*" One consequence of the current CPS system is that some parents who never learn to be competent parents, and never learn to make the significant life changes that would maintain their children's happiness, health, growth, and development, instead learn only how to get out of the system.

THE IMPORTANCE OF APPEARING EARNEST

Did CPS caseworkers help parents deal with their problems? Some did, sometimes. Jean, always compliant with caseworkers and interventionists, said she knew from the outset why CPS intervened on behalf of her children and was aware of their expectations. Other parents seemed less clear about the reasons for CPS involvement. Some, like Pauline, seemed able to address their problems independent of CPS intervention. Many parents feared possible repercussions, so they were not always honest with caseworkers about their problems. Ann said she trusted her second caseworker and advocated honest relationships. How, she asked rhetorically, could she obtain the help she needed if she couldn't be honest about her problems? She expressed mistrust for her first caseworker, however, saying she feared telling the truth about her depression and her husband's drinking and violence because she thought CPS would take her child again. She portrayed some parents in the program as angry and mistrustful, and said they viewed the program as "stupid," but also spoke with candor about their denial of having maltreated their children:

> We all didn't get here because we didn't do anything. And you will hear people say, "I didn't abuse my children." Well, something got you involved with Child Protective Services. You won't hear a lot of people admit that there's a potential for child abuse, or, "Yes, I might have done it, but I didn't mean to do it." You don't hear that. You just hear denial, denial, denial. I'm willing to admit that there is a potential for abuse, and there is a problem.

Counter to my expectations, every parent I interviewed eventually told me they believed that CPS was justified in intervening in their lives. Although one can never be absolutely certain of the sincerity of another person, I believed that Ann and Pauline recognized that the parenting they provided their children was inadequate. Jean's track record for honesty made me doubt her sincerity, although she was the first to admit that her children should have been removed from her custody. Admitting that there was a problem did not mean help was forthcoming, however. Ann waited months for counseling and for drug and alcohol treatment. Feeling desperate, she called her caseworker weekly from a pay phone—while she tried to keep her toddler from running into a busy street—to request services that were unavailable, despite the fact that they had been ordered by the court. Four months into the study, I asked Ann how she was going to get out of the system. Ann responded that unless she received help, she never would. Ann recognized that unless she was honest about her problems, she would not get the help she needed, but as long as she was honest, Ann said, "Child Protective Services will never see me as quite fit to parent."

Parents' frustrations, lack of skills, and profound relationship disturbances were catalysts for their involvement in CPS, but CPS involvement, rather than alleviating problems, created additional stress, according to parents and staff. Staff members of the Parenting Program believed caseworkers needed to increase advocacy for families and to help them find and access needed services that would help address the problems that brought them to CPS. They believed that rather than advocating for parents, many caseworkers asked parents to "jump through hoops."

Because most of the parents in the program were unemployed and living in poverty, a major challenge was finding them adequate housing and arranging some kind of income for them, usually Aid to Families with Dependent Children (AFDC) payments, prior to their children's return. The catch was that parents couldn't receive AFDC monies unless they had custody of their children, and they couldn't regain custody of their children until they had housing, furniture, and so on. One parent called to tell me she had finally made arrangements with welfare and her children were going to be returned to her custody. She had called her attorney, who contacted her caseworker and insisted that the caseworker write a letter on the parent's behalf—a courtesy that had not been offered prior to the attorney's intervention.

Staff members believed many parents became better parents following intervention. They believed others, however, simply mastered the game, by learning to comply with instructions and to say what they believed their caseworkers wanted to hear. Some parents left the system, but questions about the welfare of their children remained. None of the three women in this book succeeded in escaping the poverty, violence, and isolation that contributed to their involvement in the system.

Pauline faced new hardships but seemed to maintain the integrity of her family through each of them. Pauline took Cody and moved in with her boyfriend when her mother's mental illness resurfaced. It was rumored that Pauline's boyfriend sexually molested Cody, and that she left him and was once again on her own, but that she and Cody were doing all right. CPS closed the cases of other families as well, but they did not remain outside the system. Rumors circulated that shortly after Jean's case was closed, she deposited several of her children with various friends and relatives and departed for Las Vegas with her drug-addicted boyfriend and her favorite daughter. A year later, she was rumored to have returned and to have become involved again with CPS. Ann, involved with CPS a second time with her second child, kept in touch with me for several years. Despite her intelligence, perseverance, and desire to have a "normal family," she never was able to maintain adequate parenting skills or master the game.

NO WAY OUT

Throughout the 2 years I knew Ann, painful interactions with her family persisted, but although Ann's life seemed to be a succession of family problems and personal crises, other parts of her life seemed ordinary. I recall the tour of her garden she gave me the first time I visited her two-bedroom apartment. The apartment complex consisted of a series of undistinguished, two-story brown boxes, but in front of Ann's building there was a small plot of land about 2' × 3' where she had planted green beans, zinnias, and marigolds. She tended them daily, watering and weeding, until a profusion of buds waited to blossom. Her worn but clean apartment had pictures on the walls, and Ben's toys were gathered in orderly piles. She talked of her plans to hang blinds in the front window and buy a screen door. I could smell fresh paint during one visit — Ann had just painted her kitchen and was excited to show it to me. But the orderliness she brought to her garden and apartment was not as easily achieved in other areas of her life.

Ann experienced frequent momentous changes in her life throughout the year of this study, as did most parents in the program. Like her relationship with her parents, Ann's relationship with her husband was painful and unsettled. One afternoon, a few weeks after I first visited her apartment, I approached Ann as she stood in an alley behind the church with other parents. Lighting a cigarette, she told us in a low, monotone voice that her husband had just spent his $300 paycheck on camping gear and had driven away in his car. It was the sixth of the month, and their apartment rent, television rent, and electricity bill had not been paid.

Ann called Aid to Families with Dependent Children (AFDC or

"welfare") and learned that she must wait 30 days from the date her husband left before she could receive money. Because she had no money and knew no one from whom she could borrow any, she gathered a few personal belongings and took them to sell at her mother-in-law's garage sale. She earned $50 for food, but there wasn't enough for rent and utilities. Whenever she saw a television repair truck drive by that month, she was "sure they were coming to repossess her TV." An eviction notice from her landlord was a prerequisite for receiving emergency rent funds, but another parent recommended that Ann approach her landlord, explain the situation, and ask for an eviction notice rather than wait until she received one "because by then the landlord has had it."

One morning, Ann called from the welfare office. She immediately apologized for calling, then asked if I would drive her and Ben to the social security office. I asked for the address, and she left to ask someone. As I waited on the phone, I heard Ann speak to Ben first in a gentle, firm voice, and then in a raw, pleading voice, telling him not to hurt another child whose loud protests were followed by a chorus of squeals and cries.

When I arrived at the welfare office, Ann and Ben were waiting outside the stark, one-story cement block government building. We loaded Ben's stroller in the back of my station wagon, situated Ben in the back seat, and fastened his safety belt. As she sat in the front seat next to me, Ann told me that an employee at the AFDC office had suggested that she attend parenting classes. She hated her husband, she told me, for what he was doing to her. That morning she had awakened too late to catch the bus and keep her welfare appointment; so with baby and stroller in tow, Ann had hitchhiked to the welfare office. They could not take time to eat and chance missing the appointment. They had neither the money nor the time to eat out or to catch a bus home before their next appointment — and missed appointments might mean missed meals in the future.

In addition to daily struggles, Ann suffered from recurring bouts of depression that affected her ability to parent, and Ben was a challenging child to parent. Ben was known as "Bam Bam" by teachers at the therapeutic preschool program he attend. His constant activity demanded a great deal of energy from caregivers. A handsome child who loved socializing with adults and children, Ben's repertoire also included a number of behaviors not appreciated by others including biting, hitting, screaming, and arching his back if someone attempted to pick him up when he did not want to move. Some staff members speculated that Ben might have diagnosable fetal alcohol effects and wondered if his behavior could be attributed to prenatal exposure to drugs or alcohol.

Whatever the underlying causes of Ann's depression, alcoholism, and drug addictions, and Ben's behavior problems, Ann and Ben had few familial resources to help them meet the everyday demands of their lives. Ann turned instead to Parenting Program staff. Throughout her life, when Ann needed help, family was inaccessible, so she relied on agencies rather than relatives. I recall looking through her family photo album as she pointed to pictures of counselors, social workers, and professionals from the agencies and institutions that had taken the place of Ann's family from the time she was 16.

At one time she hoped that Mike would be the answer, "You know, I thought, 'Mike's got a family,' and I thought maybe I found a family. No, that would have been too easy. I have to have a neurotic mother-in-law, a gay brother-in-law, and they are all drunks." Without education, money, family, or close friends — those things that foster self-sufficiency, or at least make one seem self-sufficient — Ann could count only social service agencies among her resources. And social services could be counted as resources only during working hours and when staff were available and willing.

Ann's separation from Mike was brief. She allowed him to return, and she enrolled in school to earn a nurse's aide certificate. Mike's drinking and violence escalated, so she and Ben fled to temporary sheltered housing for battered women. Ann left school without graduating. The time she and Ben were permitted to live in the shelter ended, and she was forced to move into the only affordable apartment she could find.

The second-floor apartment was located in a part of town notorious for drugs and crime. It was the kind of neighborhood where a child at play would seldom be watched by a friendly neighbor; residents took no pride in their surroundings, and few remained long enough to establish lasting relationships. I first visited the apartment a week before Christmas. Passing a man whose stare made me uneasy, I knocked on the door and watched as old drapes were pulled aside a few inches. Ann peered out, checking to see who was there before opening the door. A suffocating wall of hot air that radiated from a baseboard heater made me stop short as the door opened, and I drew in a final breath of fresh outdoor air before I stepped inside. Ann wrapped her arms tightly around me and held me for what seemed like minutes.

A tired, sagging double bed occupied a full quarter of the single-room apartment, and a dresser with a rented television on it, a dilapidated reclining chair that had seen years of sitting, a scarred end table and lamp, and Ben's toys, piled in one corner, occupied most of the remainder of the room. A bathroom, closet, and closet-sized space that served as a kitchen, although it lacked appliances, comprised the remainder of the apartment. Tattered, dingy drapes hanging unevenly from the only window maintained Ann and Ben's privacy but also obstructed daylight making the apartment feel small and close.

Ben was asleep on the bed, and we sat carefully so not to awaken him. Ann described the difficulties she faced in making ends meet. Mike wasn't helping with money, and their apartment was too small for raising a child, especially one as active as Ben. The apartment had no holiday decorations, but the Community Program made certain that Ben received gifts from Santa. Ann and I spoke for a short time, and she shared mostly bad news. We vowed to talk again after the holidays.

One evening 2 months later Ann called from her apartment where she sat alone with an unopened bottle of wine. Ben was at the home of a babysitter who was provided by her drug and alcohol treatment program so that she could attend evening meetings. It was rainy and cold and they had spent most of their time in the apartment recently because Ben had been sick with asthma during the previous 3½ months. "I'm afraid I'll hurt him," she said. Ann related bits and pieces of information about the events troubling her. When Ann's friend took them to lunch, Ben threw a tantrum and broke the handle on his new car. Ann directed her friend to take them to the Parenting Program office where she walked in and announced to staff members that she couldn't handle Ben and was going to leave him there.

Crying softly, she described feelings of inadequacy. She told me she had hit Ben with her fists, then assured me she hit him only on his legs. "Oh, Ann," I pleaded, "Don't hit your child." "I know," she said with frustration in her voice. I asked if it helped, and if he behaved better, when she hit Ben. "It doesn't help," she told me, "and it's terrible to hear him, 'You hurt me, you hurt me.' I'll tell him, 'I'm sorry,' and he says, 'Thank you, Mama.'" She cried harder and said, "I'm just like my dad, and I know it, and I hate it." I asked her if she had told Isabelle and she said 'yes,' which I later confirmed when several staff members from the program told me about the same incident. I felt helpless, but relieved that I wouldn't have to file a report to CPS.

We talked about the things that Ann might do to help reduce the stress and frustration she felt. She couldn't afford to attend school so that she could get a "decent job" because she would lose welfare money. She received $369 each month and spent $235 on rent. There was not enough money remaining each month to pay for groceries. Orchestrating a move, paying more rent, and paying tuition were impossible. No matter what she tried, "there was always a barrier." Several times she told me that she felt afraid, "I think of dying too much, feeling like there's no way out."

After our conversation, I thought, perhaps Ann is right. Perhaps there is no way out. Strategies are available to help parents acquire knowledge about parenting. Parents said the program did a good job of that. But her need to learn parenting skills was only one of Ann's problems. As time passed, she commented that with most of her problems, the Parenting Program couldn't help her. Ann lived a monotonous stream of days in an apartment that measured 10' × 16', feeling pain from teeth she couldn't afford to fix, caring for a challenging child who had no space to play, receiving threats but no money from her ex-husband, and seeking almost constant medical attention for Ben, whose asthma worsened during stressful situations. The parenting skills Ann demonstrated in the program disintegrated as her situation outside the program deteriorated.

But Ann's story differed greatly according to the moment of its telling. Two months after Ann called me as she sat with an unopened bottle of wine, she had completed 4 weeks of school toward her nurse's aide certificate. The program helped her find resources to pay tuition, and she had scored four As, a B, and a C on her tests. She was surprised and proud that she could succeed in school after so many years. Ann was less depressed than usual after she began taking medication for her depression. She had doubled her dosage without consulting her physician, however, and was having difficulty remaining awake and alert. Ben was seeing a play therapist because of his aggressive behavior. Ann had bruises in the shapes of Ben's teeth covering her forearms. Ann had used the telephone book to locate an attorney who provided a free first visit and accepted payments, and she planned to file for custody of Ben. She did not seem concerned about the $750 attorney's fee, despite the fact that she had to choose each month between food and diapers because she could not afford both. Ann was optimistic that this time she would make it — get a good job, regain custody of Ben, and close her CPS case.

Ann seemed happier than at any other time during the year I had known her, but I knew that by the time of our next conversation her life might have again changed drastically. The changes in her life were almost always crises that brought her to a new agency or prolonged her association with an agency that was familiar to her. I recall the time Ann shared her family photograph album with me and the feeling of sadness that swept across me as I saw Ann's time marked by one relationship after another with some caring counselor or social worker who had temporarily become Ann's family. Ann began relying on social service agencies when she was 16 until they became—or she came to see them—as her only resources. Each agency or professional would eventually tire of her, or she would tire of them, or she would not get better or stay better long enough, or perhaps her allotted time with them would come to an end.

I did not know when I began writing the results of my research if the beginning of Ann's story would predict the end. I hoped that it wouldn't. Ann's journey had been long and tortuous, and if it was to end happily, I believed she would need to be free of what Garbarino (1990) called the "ecological conspiracies" that dominated her life. She would need things not typically offered by CPS or intervention programs: food, a job, medical care, and a safe, secure place for Ben to live, grow, and play. She would need much more than the small, narrowly defined interventions that specialists like me are so carefully trained to give. Like me, like all of us, she would need personal strength and supportive relationships that endured throughout her life.

Two years after my first observation in the Parenting Program and a year after my visit to Ann's apartment, I wrote that I had not seen or heard from Ann in 7 months. At times I would notice someone in a crowd or on the street who resembled her as when one sometimes imagines, for an instant, seeing a friend or relative who has died. I heard from program staff that Ann no longer had custody of Ben, not even for visits, and that her case was in "permanent planning," the legal process that could lead to the removal of Ben from her life completely and forever.

I recall a pleasant spring evening when Ann and I returned to her apartment after having taken Ben to dinner and to the park. We were both relieved that Ben not only had behaved during dinner but also had left the park without protest. After playing with him a short time, Ann changed Ben's diapers, and with her face a few inches from his, told him how much she loved him and gave him small, gentle kisses before singing a lullaby and tucking him into his bed. We talked for several hours that night about her childhood and family. Our candid conversation made me sad—and cognizant of the real differences in our histories, despite our common economic backgrounds. After the interview, I recorded in my notes that given her history, I wondered whether Ann would ever have a secure life or be able to provide a stable home for Ben. And now, although the question no longer seems moot, I think back to the times I saw Ann so lovingly parent her son, and I continue to wonder.

CONCLUSIONS: MAKING SENSE OF NONSENSE

The purpose of this study was to learn the views of parents involved with CPS regarding child maltreatment and the child welfare system. At the outset, I was especially interested in intervention offered by a family intervention program, the Parenting Program, and I expected to learn particulars about elements of the program parents liked and disliked. I anticipated that I would gain insight about the families enrolled and learn more about the ways parents viewed their children. Instead I learned about the parents' personal histories and their family struggles. Rather than feeling enlightened, throughout the study I felt demoralized by the seeming ineffectiveness of the system and confused by the complexity of the families' problems and the incongruence of the events and outcomes. How does one make sense of things that seem so disconnected and senseless?

The families and their situations are not surprising to those who work in the field of child welfare and are familiar with theory and research on child maltreatment. All 55 families in the Parenting Program were poor. Thirty-five parents were unemployed. Twelve families were homeless, and another 10 families lived in housing caseworkers described as inadequate. Half of the parents had not completed high school. Twenty-two parents had little or no support from family or friends. Over half had past histories or present problems with drugs or alcohol. Thirty parents had documented mental health problems. Some had developmental disabilities. The families were predictable, but also offered surprises — even to program staff.

To the Parenting Program staff members who were interviewed after reading the completed study, my description of the parents made them easily identifiable, and I was said to have captured Jean, Ann, and Pauline "to a 't.'" However, "the enormity of the troubles parents experienced in their lives" was striking to Georgia. In her words, "We know they have troubles, but when one sees one trauma after another that would break most people, it is overwhelming." One program interventionist was surprised by her own reactions to the parents' words. She thought she had been "open to families' needs" and had an "unbiased view," but the parents' stories actually allowed her to "put [herself] in their shoes." Georgia commented on the feelings of hopelessness experienced by families — feelings I too experienced at times throughout the study:

> Suicide seemed a viable option. When I listened to Ann contemplate suicide, I thought immediately, 'Here is an option.' Generally

I don't consider suicide a very good option, but I don't know what in the hell I would do. The pattern was so entrenched and intergenerational.

Parents were characterized by staff as "damaged" by their past histories and current situations. Consistent with staff's perceptions of parents, Egeland (1988) points out that the mother's history of having been abused is perhaps the most important predictor of child maltreatment. The variability among individual parents who were abused as children may result in part from mediating factors. Egeland and Erickson (1990) report that the way mothers conceptualize the care they received during childhood is more important than the actual care they received in the transmission of abusive behavior from generation to generation.

Parents who become involved with CPS agencies have huge problems — within themselves, in their relationships with others, and in their daily survival. The life circumstances of families in the program were harmful to their children. Jean, Ann, and Pauline acknowledged this and also acknowledged responsibility for their involvement with CPS. Yet the expectations of parents held by the CPS system, despite initially seeming overwhelming to parents, were ultimately small and inconsequential in comparison to the sum total of such large, intractable problems. For all the pain experienced by children and parents in this study, for all the monies invested in legal intervention and maintaining the CPS and foster care systems, for all the time and energy parents and children spent waiting and worrying, there was very little return. The CPS system does not help most children, and it harms many of them by setting criteria for "success" that have little to do with the problems that bring families to them in the first place and amount, at best, to very short term success indeed. Moreover, everyone in the study who had experience with CPS — parents, the program co-directors, family interventionists — acknowledged that intervention is inadequate.

Rather than changing the trajectory of the families' lives, the intervention offered by CPS briefly altered a predictable path to further misfortune. CPS squandered opportunities to make significant changes in the lives of parents who were so much more a part of mainstream society than I had anticipated. These were parents who wanted a "normal family," a "good job," and a "nice place to live." They were parents who regretted their lack of formal education. When I asked them what they wanted for their children, each of the three parents I interviewed told me she hoped her child or children would attend college someday. These were parents who recognized their inadequacies in parenting their children, who wanted to become better parents, and who were motivated to become better parents in order to regain the right to parent their children. Yet little was offered to help them and only for the briefest possible periods of time.

At one time during the study, Georgia reminded me that some parents in the program were successful. She suggested that perhaps the most "needy" parents volunteered for the study. After she read the results, I asked her if Jean, Ann, and Pauline were atypical parents. "At first, I want to say they are atypical," she responded, "but when I stop and think about families the way you have stopped and looked at these three families, all of them are extreme."

"It's the up and down," explained another interventionist. "When I first started, I'd see families going through the program and they would be doing really well. I would think, 'This is really working. The parent is succeeding, and the goals are being achieved, and, moreover, there is a relationship developing with the child and there is responsiveness on the parent's part.' Then in 6 months, 8 months, or a year later, they're back again with the same problems and sometimes worse."

Intervention in the Parenting Program was less successful than it appeared initially. Some parents were motivated to change, but did not know how to *be* less mentally ill, less mentally retarded, less drug addicted, less poor, or less angry. Others succeeded in meeting the minimal requirements demanded of them by the system. They demonstrated skills during the intervention program, but those skills were narrow and transient. After they exited the system, they were defeated because there was no single person or institutional entity that offered continued help or assistance—as long as they stayed out of trouble, that is. Some parents, like Ann, were unsuccessful enough to merit continued support of some kind. Some, like Pauline, used the skills they learned during intervention and structured their lives in ways that allowed their continued use. Other parents, like Jean, never really seemed to figure out what it meant to adequately parent their children, but they were savvy enough to figure out how to escape the child welfare system, if only temporarily.

Why did some parents get it right while others never did? In reality, success was rarely black and white. More often it occurred in degrees of change. Parents could demonstrate select competencies following intervention that weren't present when they started. They began to recognize their children's needs and cues and became aware that they did not always meet those needs during intervention sessions. Parents could identify people to call for help and began to recognize when they needed to request help, although help was not always available. Successes were real and important, but they were also modest and insular given the enormous problems families faced outside the carefully arranged intervention settings. Staff members believed, as does David Olds (Erickson, Egeland, Musick, & Olds, 1991), that in order for families to make lasting changes, the restructuring of relationships between children and families is paramount. Parents who are successful, according to Georgia, "see the child as someone who must be nurtured, protected, and guided." One of the program staff believed that Jean's relationship with her children was that of a peer, and that Ann "never knew what to expect" and "didn't have a clue about how children and parents interact. Ann just wanted a child to love her." In contrast, Pauline was able to prioritize her relationship with her child. When her boyfriend was suspected of harming Cody, Pauline was clear about who was more important. With many other women, Georgia said, "It's an old story. The boyfriend may have just been paroled for armed robbery, but you'll hear the mother say, 'Men like this don't come along every day.'"

The need for financial and social support by young single parents should not be discounted, however. Mothers who successfully break the cycle of abuse are likely to have an intact, stable, and satisfying relationship with a husband or boyfriend (Egeland & Erickson, 1990). Although the qualities of those women that support healthy relationships with their husbands or boyfriends may be similar to those that support healthy relationships with their children, the change in financial security that occurs when mothers are no longer single parents is also significant. When parents exit the Parenting Program and CPS, specific skills may have changed, but familial contexts have not. Georgia explained, "All the factors that created problems are still there." In the context of relating the story of a homeless mother she saw walking in the rain with her four children and a voucher for one night in a motel, Georgia asked, "How can you expect anyone to do a good job of parenting when they haven't figured out where they are going to sleep that night?" The mother, evicted from a shelter after her allotted time ended, had 24 hours to find an apartment to rent — on foot, in the rain, with her 10-year-old son carrying her infant, and two other children in tow.

What can be done for those parents and children? I was more certain before I conducted this study than I was afterward that I had the power to help families make meaningful changes for their children. My professional training is in the areas of psychology and special education, and I am skilled at changing the behavior of children and families in clinical settings. But I have come to believe that no matter how

skilled the professional in changing the behavior of parents who maltreat their children, the skills those parents acquire are likely to be
undermined by their histories and the difficult futures they will certainly face in our country.

To my genuine surprise (and dismay) there were times throughout
the study when I identified with the ways I imagined caseworkers must
feel rather than feeling empathy for the parents. Given the enormity of
the problems the parents faced but could not address and the real damage children suffered, why shouldn't CPS intervene by removing the
children from their families? Georgia stated emphatically her belief
that children should not be removed because "the state has never demonstrated it's ability to do a better job" than the families themselves.
She believes that rather than taking children from families, caseworkers
should be provided with the tools they need to perform their jobs.

> All the protective services worker can offer is the wonderful service
> of 'Well, we can remove your kids and place them in foster care, if
> we have any available.' And talk. They can provide parents with
> talk, but they don't have time to listen. They can throw out some
> advice, but that's it. Caseworkers don't have tools available.

Georgia believes that caseworkers are expected to perform their most
difficult and important jobs with their "hands tied, their feet bound"
and their voices "gagged."

Like the staff of the Parenting Program, I no longer view the problem as lying primarily with CPS. I have come to believe that the lack
of clarity in the purposes and functions of CPS is not the problem but
merely a symptom of the problem. Given the scope and characteristics
of child maltreatment as it has evolved in our society, it seems we
have asked CPS to perform an impossible task: to insure the safety and
well-being of children in a society that will not support families in the
most minimal, basic ways — by providing child care, by making sure
they receive health care, by seeing that they are educated, or even by
assuring that they sleep in houses rather than in cars, in tents, or on our
city streets.

CHANGING THE SYSTEM

How should the child welfare system change, and what tools
should be provided to change it? Staff members who reacted to the
study were clear and prompt in answering. They believed that, first,

intervention must be based on models of secondary prevention aimed at high-risk groups; it must occur prior to actual incidents of maltreatment. The current approaches most frequently used by CPS agencies are based on models of tertiary prevention that require families to fail before they are eligible to receive services. A secondary preventive approach would identify families at risk for child maltreatment and provide services aimed at interrupting future occurrences of maltreatment. Families, one interventionist explained, should be received with open arms and applause when they acknowledge their lack of parenting skills and ask for help by saying, "I'm afraid I'm going to hurt my children."

Second, program staff believed that intervention must be of sufficient duration to allow families to become, in Georgia's words, "customers," and to develop trust in the individuals and agencies offering it. They believed intervention should be so desirable that families "clamor" to receive it. Byron Egeland (Erickson, Egeland, Musick, & Olds, 1991) speaks of families' need to come and go. As changes in life situations dictate the need for support and services, those services need to be seen by families as useful and comprehensive in meeting their needs, flexible in delivery, readily available, and easily accessible. Timetables for providing services need to reflect the characteristics and dynamics of the problems they are designed to address and the lifestyles of families needing them.

Third, after reading the study, staff members stressed that intervention must be delivered by highly trained and skilled interventionists. According to Egeland, the treater is more important than the treatment (Erickson, Egeland, Musick, & Olds, 1991). Caseworkers and interventionists need skills in effective communication with families and professionals. They need knowledge of the theories and philosophies guiding various intervention approaches, and they need specific strategies for changing parent behavior. They need knowledge of family systems, child development, and parent-child interactions to assist them in accurately assessing behavior, influencing change in child and family relationships, and promoting the confidence and competence of parents in caring for their children.

Fourth, and perhaps most important to interventionists in the program, the system must begin to empower parents through family support. A shift must occur from viewing parents in the framework of a deficit model to facilitating parents' acquisition and control over service, informational, and monetary resources. Parents' strengths must be fostered. Real options for education, employment, housing, health care, and child care must be provided, and parents must be encouraged to exercise those options (Cornell Empowerment Project, undated).

Only when parents learned to advocate for their children's and family's needs, the program staff believed, could parents maintain stability in their lives.

Finally, program staff expressed the belief that support and empowerment must occur within communities rather than solely within individuals and agencies. Family relationships, informal relationships, and institutional relationships are interactive and mutually influential, as Bronfenbrenner (1977) observed over 20 years ago. These relationships are influenced by legislation, social policy and practice, economics, and cultural ideologies. If intervention continues to be focused narrowly on the perceived deficits of parents within the contexts of isolated programs or agencies, changes will continue to be meager and short lived.

When the term "the battered child" originated at a seminar sponsored by the American Academy of Pediatrics in 1961, the intent of the organization was "to gain attention and increase the desire [of pediatricians] to do something about the problem" (Kempe & Helfer, 1972, p. xi). At that time, the disadvantages of using that sensational phrase were thought to be definitional, that is, the term lacked clarity and might be interpreted differently by different groups of people (Kempe & Helfer, 1972). The disadvantages have been much greater and more serious. Although maltreated children have gained the attention of professionals, policymakers, and the general public, the notion of child maltreatment as synonymous with "the battered child" persists with much of the public, and the treatment of parents as perpetrators persists in the policy and practice of CPS. This narrow focus on specific acts that are considered harmful rather than the contexts of child maltreatment have resulted in interventions that are punitive to parents and children. "The language of social service," wrote Salvador Minuchin (1991), "has become the language of crime" (p. 7). I have frequently reflected on the histories of parents in the study, their lack of having received early therapeutic treatment, and their involvement in the type of child welfare intervention that Minuchin (1991) has described as "a process of destruction" (p. 7). I have pondered the future of these parents' children and their children's children, and I fear their future and ours.

Our society has constructed a definition of child maltreatment that is related to and influenced by societal problems, but we have abdicated the responsibility for addressing the societal problems that mediate, influence, support, and perpetuate child maltreatment. As often as those of us in education and social services profess to be guided by Bronfenbrenner's ecological model, our models and interventions invariably focus on the immediate behaviors of children or families, and we fail to consider the societal and cultural contexts in which families struggle to survive. We treat child maltreatment as an abstraction rather than as a complex constellation of problems that are relative to our "feelings, values, and priorities" (Bellah, Madsen, Sullivan, Swidler, & Tipton, 1985, p. 132). We "escape from the debate" and abandon the search for social justice and equity to the small successes that result from our discrete professional interventions (Edgar, 1991, p. 10).

As a society, we will never be successful in preventing child maltreatment as long as the problems of children and families are reduced to simplistic phrases and supported by simplistic notions and until *their* problems are recognized as being *our* problems and joint responsibility is assumed for finding solutions. We are all responsible for the one-quarter of the children in our nation who live in poverty. We are responsible for their hunger, their isolation, their illness, their pain, their degradation. We have the resources to act, but we lack the will. We are not willing to implicate ourselves, accept responsibility, and take the action necessary to change the lives of the children we seek to protect. We cannot take care of the children in our nation unless we also take care of their families. And unless we begin to care for all children and families, we will not be able to continue to care for ourselves, our children, and our families. Our legacy will be more ignorance, poverty, spiritual decay, and violence.

Nicholas Anastasiow (1986) borrowed the following words of American philosopher and educator John Dewey to close a keynote speech in which he defended early intervention for young children at risk. It serves as a fitting warning about our collective future if we, as a nation, elect to continue down the path we currently travel.

> What the best and wisest parent wants for his own child, that must be what the community wants for all its children. Any other idea from our society is narrow and unlovely; acted upon it destroys democracy (p. 104).

CHAPTER 7

AFTERWORD: REFLECTIONS
ON CHANGE

It is April, 1993, 2 years after I completed the study that is presented in this book. The problems I wrote about then are more compelling to me now, as I believe they are to others too, than they were when I began my study. Last month, I taught a continuing education class to early childhood special educators, administrators, and therapists practicing in the public schools. During a discussion about the challenges of working with families living in difficult life circumstances, I asked how many participants in the class ever considered quitting their jobs. As I scanned the room, nearly every hand was raised including mine. What would trigger this kind of a response from people who were investing their time, money, and interest in developing skills to work with high risk and developmentally disabled infants and young children? The class met on Friday evenings and all day Saturdays; the participants are obviously dedicated professionals. I am certain that it is not an issue of compensation or prestige. Professionals who enter the field of early childhood intervention do not do so in order to gain money or power. Rather, work with young children and families seems to attract people who are kind and generous, people motivated by a sincere desire to help children succeed in life. I think the teachers, therapists, and administrators in my class entertained the notion of leaving their professions because, like me, they believe they cannot help the children and families with whom they work. They feel powerless to effect change, and changing things for children is their reason for being in their professions.

The situations human service professionals encounter every day, like the situations described in this book, are unsettling. Our society feels increasing angst about the nation's social and economic conditions. We want things to be different. During recent state and national elections, candidates ran for office on platforms of change. People yearn for resolutions to the disturbing situations described in this book and those they encounter during the course of daily life in our society. It is not surprising that Brian Ellerbeck, my editor, asked me to include this final chapter on change. Thus I find myself in the uncomfortable position of writing a chapter on how to go about changing a system when I waver in my belief that significantly changing the system is possible.

Let me amend my last statement. I do believe that change is possible, even that it is inevitable. However, I am skeptical about the ability of cumbersome, bureaucratic systems to engage in the type of critical self-examination and authentic dialogue that I believe is required for positive interorganizational change to occur. As an administrator at a university, engaged in work that is supposed to be about effecting systems change through university-community and agency partnerships, I am a professional meeting-goer. During meetings, inside the university and out, I vacillate between feeling disliked and discounted if I speak openly and honestly, and feeling like I am at the table in the final chapter of *Animal Farm*: "The creatures outside looked from pig to man, and from man to pig, and from pig to man again; but already it was impossible to say which was which" (Orwell, 1946, p. 128).

THE WHY OF CHANGE

Despite fleeting feelings of being too powerless or corrupted to effect positive changes myself, I believe that change in the way child welfare is viewed and fostered is imperative. How, then, will change occur? To organize my thoughts about change, I refer again to the structure hypothesized by Bronfenbrenner (1977) and discuss change within the context of the micro-, meso-, eco-, and macrosystem levels of the ecological model that were introduced earlier in the book. This structure will allow an examination of intervention for child maltreatment within the contexts of interpersonal relationships among children and families, while acknowledging the interrelationships and transactions that occur at multiple levels and influence children and families. Healthy parents, healthy children, and healthy parent-child and family relationships within home, intervention, and community settings are worthy goals for intervention at the micro- and mesosystem levels. We have available to us a strong research base to guide us in those efforts. But to stop there, and that is where service systems usually stop, is in the words of Barbara Bowman, "counterproductive at best," and "it may be immoral" (1992, p. 105). The error in focusing only on parent-child and family relationships within family systems, although this approach is a vast improvement on focusing solely on the parent or child who has been identified as deviant, is that the problems associated with poverty and maltreatment do not arise solely from the individual;

rather, the problems reside also, and I believe primarily, within society. "We have met the enemy and he is us" (Kelly, 1992).

That statement is easier for me to make in this publication than it is in my daily professional life where so much hinges on the belief in the power of individuals to effect change and in the worth of universities and state agencies to individuals and society. As I sit in work-related meetings I often recall the childhood story about the emperor's new clothes. But even if one is brave enough to point out the emperor's nudity, or the bureaucrat's or academician's impotency, what then? The process by which change should occur is less clear to me. I have stated up front that I am not optimistic that the bureaucracies and organizations with which I work are capable of significant change, and that even if they are, a shift in their collective beliefs, assumptions, and practices surely is not sufficient in and of itself to effect significant societal change.

The possibility of broad change is enhanced, I believe, through increased understanding in the general society of the reasons that change is needed. This requires a shift in the way deviance is defined by society and in the extent to which society sees itself as part of rather than apart from the deviance. The key to change, I believe, lies in large part through people's enlightenment about the perspectives of others. Through the sharing of perspectives, a new understanding, and more importantly, a revision of the way children and families are viewed in our society is possible. I further believe this kind of awareness and redefinition is more likely to occur through media such as art, literature, music, and drama, and through human interchange between those in positions of power and those with a vested interest in positive change, than through academic publications or bureaucratic meetings. I suspect that an understanding of poverty, human differences, sorrow, institutionalized malpractice, human disregard, and individual caring about humanity is more likely to result from reading Anne Frank, John Steinbeck, Charles Dickens, or Ken Kesey than it is from watching the swiftly moving, numbing stream of human suffering presented on the nightly news or reading the numbers that represent the infant mortality rate, homeless families, or children in poverty. We have grown used to hearing abbreviated news or statistics about people in crisis that do little to move us to act, but would be horrifying if we witnessed firsthand the human tragedy that lies behind those numbers. Increased understanding rather than judging will precipitate change and help us to determine the course that change should take. "The best way to control people is to encourage them to be mischievous . . . let them do what they want, and watch them. This is the best policy" (Suzuki, 1992,

p. 32). Increased understanding of child maltreatment is possible through listening to the parents in this book and seeing how they construct and interpret the world, by pondering our differences and our samenesses, our unshared circumstances and our shared humanity.

This final chapter is linked then to the substance of this book; to the stories of Jean, Ann, and Pauline. The approach I use is to observe, interpret, and reflect rather than to direct. If I must choose a paradigm to describe this approach — and no good social scientist should be without a paradigm in the 1990s, I then will stick with the interpretivist paradigm with which I started to examine child maltreatment — the reality constructed by those who experience it. (I confess that I have only a superficial understanding of Thomas Kuhn's [1970] discussions of paradigms in *The Structure of Scientific Revolutions,* so I conveniently beg the issue of paradigm selection with the excuse that a discussion about paradigms might dissuade from reading this book the audience I most want to reach. If you are a reader who desires to know more about paradigms, I refer you to Kuhn or to a thoughtful presentation and discussion by Skrtic [1991].)

My reflections about problems and issues related to children, families, and society have been shaped by the views in the works of others (Jonathan Kozol, Uri Bronfenbrenner, Arnold Sameroff, Edward Zigler, Kathryn Barnard, C. Everett Koop, Nicholas Anastasiow, Barbara Bowman, and Marian Wright Edelman, to name a few), and more intimate conversations and interactions with Diane Bricker, Casandra Firman, Ruth Kaminski, Margaret Lord, Barbara Woodward, Mike Guralnick, and especially Peggy Veltman, Gene Edgar, and Mary Carr. Most importantly, my thoughts are provoked by the perspectives of those with firsthand knowledge about child maltreatment. So let us first talk about who they are.

Food Basket Recipients

The "them" and "us" of the parents and CPS workers in this book have a parallel in society. In this book I talk about the people in poverty. It is probably apparent that I am not one of those people, and you probably are not one of them either. We are the givers of food baskets, they are the recipients. As long as we see ourselves as the givers, we will see them as the receivers. Receiving a food basket may help their families eat, but it is not the same for them as having their own supply of food. When they have their own supply of food, then they are part of us. When we give them food, they are not. When they have their own food, they make decisions about what to eat and when. When we give them food, it makes us feel good, magnanimous. It is somehow different than sharing our food with friends and loved ones, without rules or expectations attached. Rather, our giving is based on the presumption that we know what they want and need, and we may make misjudgments based on our misperceptions of them. How different are they from the rest of us?

One obvious difference is that they abuse their children and they lie about it. However, it has already been stated that abuse occurs across socioeconomic levels, although to what extent we are unsure since it is typically dealt with — or not dealt with — within the immediate family among families from middle and upper socioeconomic levels. Among families from lower socioeconomic levels it is more likely to be dealt with by systems outside the family; therefore, the definition of abuse is confounded by whether or not one gets caught. It is not clear, then, that Ann, Jean, and Pauline are different from the rest of us solely on the basis of whether or not they abused their children.

However, there is still the matter of dishonesty. Several readers of early drafts of this book expressed concern about the honesty of the three parents in general, and about Jean's penchant for prevarication in particular. If these abusive parents present themselves in a favorable light, so goes the rationale, they must be trying to trick us into believing they are something they are not. I believe there is another plausible explanation for any dishonesty, if indeed there was intentional dishonesty. (There were admittedly a number of inconsistencies between my observations and interpretations and theirs.) Perhaps the parents want to be seen as part of the mainstream of society. Perhaps they define themselves as normal or deviant by the same general criteria that are used by the rest of us, and perhaps they want to be seen in the best possible light because they want to be seen as belonging. I recall being really surprised twice during this study: once when all three parents told me they wanted their children to go to college, and a second time when all three parents admitted their culpability in being involved with CPS and their belief that they were bad parents. Why should these experiences be so surprising to me? Because in some sense I viewed the three parents as different from me and outside the mainstream of society. But are they? They view success in much the same ways as the rest of us — as owning a home and a car, and being able to send one's children to college. The degree to which those dreams are possible for individuals in our society may be the biggest difference between "us" and "them."

My friend and colleague Mary Carr hypothesizes that there are three general categories of people who live in poverty. The first group is the newly poor. This group suffers from contemporaneous problems such as economic downturns or changes in employment opportunities like the closing of lumber mills, automobile plants, or military bases. The second group is part of a second generation of poverty due in large part to the breakdown of available extended family and community to help people ride out the waves and troughs of the life events experienced by the first group. The third group includes families in society's "underclass," that is, those who are experiencing intergenerational, protracted poverty (Auletta, 1983). We can afford to look much more closely at the third group than the first two because the differences between them and us are greater; the differences are behavioral as well as economic. The people in this group are clearly different from us. The first two groups are more troublesome. If we dare to believe what Jonathan Kozol (1988) writes in *Rachel and Her Children,* that people can work and own homes one day and lose everything in a fire the next day and never recover, then we also must believe that tragedy can happen to us.

It is important to remember that people living in poverty cannot be characterized accurately in one way. Individuals and circumstances vary greatly. Nor do these three categories of poverty suffice to explain the phenomena, but perhaps they serve to blur the line we see between "them" and "us."

Just as not all people in poverty are the same, not all people in poverty maltreat their children. One does not have to be poor to maltreat or be maltreated, nor does one have to be poor to suffer an unfavorable developmental, educational, or life outcome. Incidents of reported child maltreatment are much higher among impoverished people, however, and maltreatment does result in behavioral and developmental differences and delays that cannot be attributed solely to poverty. It is also true that among families in society's underclass there are behavioral as well as income deficiencies. Behavioral problems among people in poverty may be real enough and may need to be changed in order to maintain some sort of societal balance and to foster child welfare, but judgments about differences among people are not particularly helpful in alleviating problems and improving situations for children. Let us be clear about what it is we want for children in our nation and, if we must judge, let us judge society's abdication of responsibility for our social and moral ecology. Then let us get about the business of translating our dissatisfactions into actions that are useful and fruitful.

The Concept of Risk

A model that I believe to be useful in understanding the relationship between risk conditions and outcomes and that is applicable to issues of child welfare was articulated in 1976 by Tjossem. The three risk categories he used to describe vulnerable children have been used to guide research, to develop high-risk infant identification and developmental monitoring systems in a number of states, and to serve as the basis for defining populations eligible for early intervention services under the Part H Amendments to the Education for All Handicapped Children Act of 1986 (which was reauthorized subsequently as the Individuals with Disabilities Education Act). The three risk conditions that Tjossem used to describe vulnerable children are:

> *Established risk.* Established risk infants are those whose early appearing aberrant development is related to diagnosed medical disorders of known etiology bearing relatively well-known expectancies for developmental outcome within specified ranges of developmental delay. The Down's syndrome infant is a classic example of established risk. The early medical, educational, and social interventions employed with these children are aimed at aiding them to develop and function at the higher end of the range for their limiting disorder.
>
> *Environmental risk.* Environmental risk applies to biologically sound infants for whom early life experiences including maternal and family care, health care, opportunities for expression of adaptive behaviors, and patterns of physical and social stimulation are sufficiently limiting to the extent that, without corrective intervention, they impart high probability for delayed development.
>
> *Biological risk.* Biological risk specifies infants presenting history of prenatal, perinatal, neonatal, and early development events suggestive of biological insult(s) to the developing central nervous system and which either single or collectively, increase the probability of later appearing aberrant development. Early diagnosis of enduring developmental fault is often difficult and inconclusive of these biologically vulnerable infants who, most often, require close surveillance and modified care during the early developmental years (p. 5).

These categories of risk are not mutually exclusive; rather they are dynamic and mutually influential. Infants and children move between categories of normalcy (e.g., good health and typical developmental patterns) and deviance (e.g., atypical physical, functional, or behavioral developmental patterns) in large part because of environmental mediators — especially parental education and socioeconomic status.

The term "risk" refers to probabilistic rather than cause-and-effect relationships (Pianta, 1990). The consequences of risk conditions are by no means immutable; there is great variance in child outcomes. This is hardly startling news. These concepts of risk have been commonly accepted not only among academics, they are reflected in federal policy. Biological and environmental risk conditions were incorporated into Public Law 99.457, Part H in addition to established conditions, so that high-risk children could receive services *before* they developed handicapping conditions. What is news is that the importance of preventive approaches to the attenuation or mitigation of the powerful mediating effect of the environment on the developing child continues to be largely ignored in policy and practice at state and program levels in the areas of health, education, and child welfare.

It's Hard to Get In, and It's Hard to Get Out

It is suspicious that children and families of color and those who live in poverty are identified more readily for the "bad services," services that result in punitive intervention, than they are for the "good services," services designed to support and promote child and family health and development. In a study of special education in five urban school systems conducted by Palfrey, Singer, Walker, and Butler (1987), the age at which children's developmental problems were diagnosed varied according to the type, severity, and complexity of the condition. Low-incidence, more severe disabling conditions (such as Down's syndrome or cerebral palsy) were identified earlier than high-incidence disabilities that are inferred from low performance (such as mild mental retardation or speech and language delays) (Edgar, 1988). It is not surprising that more visible differences are easier to detect than subtle differences. Of greater interest is the finding of Palfrey and colleagues that the age at which developmental problems were identified was related to diagnosis by a physician, that is, physicians detected problems earlier than non-physicians. The researchers also found that children with better educated mothers were usually diagnosed earlier than those with poorly educated mothers, and that children who were white and lived in families of middle and upper incomes were identified earlier than children of color who were living in poverty.

So, children born to educated parents in middle- and upper-income families are more likely to have a relationship with a physician who knows the child and family personally and a "medical home that provides primary health care services, comprehensive in nature, which address the needs of the whole child" (Sia & Breakey, 1985). The parents may be better at recognizing developmental differences and communicating them to professionals, and the professionals may be more willing to listen to the parents' concerns. The result of early identification, at least under ideal conditions, is comprehensive early intervention that includes an array of services designed to meet the comprehensive needs of the child and family at risk: educational, medical, nutritional, social, therapeutic, and case management services.

Contrast the scenario of the child born into an educated middle-class family with that of many children of families in poverty. Most poor children do not receive periodic, regular health care and developmental surveillance, therefore, emerging health, nutrition, developmental, and caregiving problems go undetected and untreated. At age 3, a small portion of eligible children attend Head Start programs. One might reason based on this approach to intervention that poor families do all right until their children's 3rd birthday, or that children are incapable of learning before their 3rd birthday, or perhaps that the best approach to take with children in poverty is to wait and see just how bad things can get before we take action. That seems to be the case with the majority of intervention programs, as is evident from earlier descriptions of the events experienced by families in the study and the prominence of people in poverty and people of color in the child welfare system. You must "fail" in order to become eligible for services — you must be mentally retarded, chronically ill, abuse or neglect your child, and so forth. That's the system — it is hard to get in; one needs a label that may be stigmatizing, dehumanizing, and difficult to escape. Once in, it is hard to get out.

Toward Models of Prevention

Alternative models that promote healthy growth and development have been proposed in the fields of public health, mental health, and education (Offord, 1982; Simeonsson, 1991). Robert Pianta (1990) argues eloquently that preventive services are a viable alternative to the reform of special and regular education, and that they should be viewed as expanding the scope of rather than replacing remedial programs. I propose that Pianta's argument for a preventive approach be extended to include the reform of child welfare as well as educational systems.

A preventive approach is based on the notion that it is better to strengthen the general public and inoculate them against agents that we know are problem causing than to wait until problems appear and attempt to remediate them. Pianta gives the examples of providing preventive child health care and immunizations and fluoridating drinking water to prevent cavities in children. These are widely accepted primary preventive practices.

Secondary preventive approaches are offered to groups of people who are more likely to experience some kind of poor outcome than the general population, such as poor school performance or early school withdrawal among children in poverty or HIV/AIDS among people with multiple sexual partners. Examples of secondary prevention approaches include Head Start, nutrition counseling for young women of childbearing age with phenylketonuria, and school dropout prevention programs. This approach targets particular high-risk groups that did not receive primary prevention or did not change in desired or expected ways as a result of primary prevention.

Tertiary preventive approaches offer intervention after poor outcomes occur, "that is, after the child has failed" (Pianta, 1990, p. 308). The goal of tertiary prevention is remediation of the adverse consequences of a disorder or an undesirable outcome. Special education programs and CPS programs are examples of tertiary prevention approaches. Of great relevance to discussions about child welfare is the following observation by Pianta (1990): "Relative to prevention-oriented systems for which eligibility rules do not mandate failure, remedial service delivery systems increase the distance between the child's level of competence at entry to the system (failure), and the level of competence acceptable for exit from the system (average performance). Recognition of this fact leads to the conclusion that remedial services, *in the absence of preventive services*, may actually increase the likelihood of failure" (p. 309).

Models of primary and secondary prevention are inclusive, rather than exclusive like the tertiary prevention model. They are presumably less stigmatizing and less punitive because they do not require a criterion or judgment of failure to allow people to receive services. They occur earlier in the course of the development of the person or problem; therefore, the distance people must travel to succeed is shorter and their problems are less intractable. The only meaningful and viable approach to the care of children is one that utilizes primary and secondary approaches to prevention and intervention. Primary and secondary prevention and intervention approaches, using Tjossem's inclusive and dynamic definitions of risk would enable us to identify those children whose welfare needs protection before illness, abuse, or school failure has occurred. Once identified, those children should receive comprehensive, integrated, individualized, continuous, and universally accessible intervention that addresses all the possible outcomes of risk including poor health, delayed general development, deficient educational achievement, and maltreatment.

THE HOW OF CHANGE

Despite their making intuitive sense to some people, early, comprehensive, integrated, universally accessible, individualized, and continuous intervention approaches are perceived by many others to be more expensive than the fractionated approaches we now use in our attempt to ensure the health, education, and social welfare of children in our country. After all, early, comprehensive models might result in some undeserving child or family getting health care, child care, education, food, or housing they do not really need, and it is always possible that we will provide services to some children and families and they will turn out badly despite our interventions. (I tried using a similar argument with my mother when I was about age 5 to get out of making my bed because it would get messed up again anyway when I slept in it. I assume you, like my mother, can generate alternative arguments for making beds and taking care of children and families.)

What do early, integrated, universal, individualized, and continuous intervention approaches look like? Health care, day care, education, food, and housing that is universally available and accessible and is of high quality. We know how to deliver quality programs, but we are not willing to fund and mandate quality. Head Start programs, for example, have received nonpartisan political support and continuously increasing funds, and they are widely believed to be effective in reversing adverse trends in the physical, social, and intellectual development of children in poverty. However, Head Start programs are inadequately funded given the variety and levels of intervention and services needed by children and families who participate in them. Head Start programs serve less than one-fifth of eligible 4- and 5-year-olds, they are often staffed by personnel who are neither qualified nor competent, and they result in limited and short-term changes in children's intellectual functioning. The above statements do not negate the significant contributions of Head Start in providing respite care for families and nutrition and health care for children, increasing the social competence of children, and acting as a catalyst for improvements in the school and health care systems (Zigler, 1990).

The quality of Head Start programs is not the primary issue here, but an example I am using to point out a larger issue. Service programs and agencies frequently find themselves in the position of wanting to do good things for children and families, but they lack the awareness, knowledge, skills, and resources necessary to replicate models that have demonstrated success, or they lack the knowledge and skills necessary to evaluate their own performance and adjust intervention approaches to more adequately support positive child and family outcomes. The competitive grant process in our country results in the development of truly outstanding models of intervention (e.g., the Yale Child Welfare Research Program [Rescorla, Provence, & Naylor, 1983]; the Carolina Abecedarian Project [Ramey & Campbell, 1984]; Project CARE [Ramey, Bryant, Sparling, & Wasik, 1985]; the Infant Health and Development Project [Gross, Speiker, Casey, Brooks-Gunn, & Ramey, 1990]) that have demonstrated important changes in the developmental status of children and life circumstances of families and contributed greatly to our knowledge base about what can be accomplished. These models are outstanding but the knowledge gained from them is diminished because the knowledge base is not translated into action in policy development, fiscal planning and responsibility, information dissemination, and continued on-site support and assistance in the application of principles and strategies. Funding, training, dissemination, and programs are diluted to the point where models cannot be replicated with fidelity, therefore, they are ineffective in producing positive outcomes. This phenomenon is referred to in Washington State as "model rich and resource poor." It is not a lack of commitment to children and families at the service delivery level that keeps us from acting on our knowledge, it is a lack of monetary and personnel resources dedicated to carrying out the actions we know can benefit children and families.

It is relatively easy to identify strategies at micro- and mesosystem levels that will effectively promote and support the healthy growth, development, and well-being of children — and the competence and confidence of their families — although researchers will argue the finer points. Past policies governing the resources allocated to higher education and monies for demonstration programs supported the proliferation of academic entrepreneurs in our nation capable of developing and evaluating model programs. We are rich in this regard relative to many other nations; however, we lack the commitment demonstrated by other nations in developing broad policies and funding programs that capitalize on our knowledge and talents.

At the microsystem level, strategies that have demonstrated success in promoting child health, safety, and development, as well as in supporting optimal parent-child interactions, should be applied by all professionals and by all programs that interface with children and families. Child welfare is not just a concern of the child welfare system. There is not a teacher, physician, nurse, social worker, or clergy member who has not been touched by issues of child welfare. Children and families reach the child welfare system after innumerable squandered opportunities throughout their lives for things to turn out better. Appropriate training in intervention approaches that have demonstrated success must be required of personnel by health, education, and social service agencies and certifying organizations at the ecosystem level. Training must be supported by state and federal funds at the macrosystem level. In my home state of Washington, teachers in public schools and preschool programs are providing early intervention services to children and families without working knowledge or skills in the areas of typical and atypical child development, parent-child interactions, or family systems. The predominant model employed in these systems is one in which the teacher-child relationship takes precedence over parent-child and family-child relationships. When families are in trouble, professionals are not equipped to help, so they transfer responsibility to caseworkers in child welfare systems who make decisions about caregiving environments but are themselves lacking in knowledge and skills in the areas of typical and atypical child development, parent-child interactions, and family systems. This scenario can be applied to professionals across agencies, disciplines, and issues — physical health, mental health, family planning, developmental disabilities. Many professionals, as well as many citizens of our nation, lack knowledge about why or how to change things even though that knowledge exists for many of the difficult situations they encounter. They only know that something is wrong and that they want it to change.

Change must be guided by the syncretism of ideas from our best and brightest citizens in the creation of intervention strategies and policies and by those who have intimate knowledge of what it is like to encounter poverty and maltreatment in our country. Change must be thoughtfully articulated and negotiated, then orchestrated and synchronized at multiple service delivery, community, and policy levels by those with the influence and control of resources to do so. Change must be desired, demanded, and then supported, through the time, money, and energy of all citizens who have a vested interest in the general health and well-being of our society. Will change occur? I leave it to you to decide. Is change possible? I am certain it is, for I have experienced it myself through the power of three parents who few would see as powerful.

PARENTS AND FAMILIES REVISITED

In April, 1989, I wrote in my research log that I felt uncertain whether or not I should have given Ann money to eat lunch one day when she and Ben were downtown keeping appointments and could not afford to eat. In May, 1989, I was unsure whether or not I should have taken bed linens to Jean's house so that she could prepare a bedroom for her children who were returning from foster care. Would these acts compromise the integrity of my research, I wondered. Shouldn't I keep my professional work and personal feelings separate? I can assure you that I feel no such ambivalence or misgivings today.

At some point the interdependence of our humanity and our professionalism must be acknowledged and reconciled. We must distinguish the research and practical, or "how," questions regarding the best ways to help children and families from the social-moral, or "should," questions regarding whether we help children and families (Anastasiow, 1986). "To do nothing is wrong, but to be thoughtless about what we do is worse" (Bowman, 1992, p. 108). Professionals must arm themselves with knowledge about the most effective and promising ways to work with children and families, and use every resource available, then let themselves off the hook because they cannot impact all aspects of the social ecology of children and families living in tragic circumstances. Professionals and families should celebrate even their smallest victories. The alternatives — to ascribe to the idea that we should not care about children or families or to believe that nothing we do can make a difference — are unthinkable.

Individuals can change and can effect change, and when ideas from diverse sources are syncretized, change is more likely to occur in the collective. My personal relationships with Ann, Jean, and Pauline profoundly impacted my life, although I doubt they have any idea that this is so. I think it must be out of the realm of their consideration to think they might have the power to influence what others think or do, yet Ann, Jean, and Pauline helped to shape my life, and they have inalterably changed my worldview. It is my hope that their stories will change the way others view child maltreatment as well, and perhaps inspire thoughtful dialogue that will lead to change in interventions and more importantly in policies that support children and families who experience violence.

We are unlikely to act to solve problems that we have not first carefully considered. Individually and collectively we are beginning to recognize how desperately bad things have become for children and families in our country; it is becoming an acceptable topic to recognize and discuss, and that makes me feel heartened because I think that the dialogue will precipitate change and is a necessary component of change. Perhaps as a result of the parents' stories your understanding of maltreatment has changed. Perhaps you are troubled by their situations and you believe they merit consideration rather than a summary judgment about the parents' guilt or innocence and a dismissal of the children once they are "safe" within the child welfare system.

Ann, Jean, and Pauline, and countless other parents and children helped me to see and to think about things in dramatically different ways than I once saw them or thought about them. When I pass angry, homeless men on the street I am less afraid of them than I once was. I feel as if I know them; they are the young children I once taught in my preschool classroom who were and continued to be neglected by their families, communities, and society. When I pass mothers and children on the street who are sad, homeless, hollow-looking, I catch their gaze and say hello. I feel a connection. In them I see Pauline, and Jean, and Ann, and I see myself.

Appendix: Methods

The methods I used to conduct the study are recounted in this appendix so that others can judge its completeness, accuracy, and trustworthiness. My relationships with the program and staff are also described, and attention is given to the implications of those relationships on my research.

This study related parents' accounts of the situations that led to their involvement with a child welfare system and the events that occurred afterward. I conducted the study in order to discover the perceptions of parents who experienced firsthand the consequences of being labeled and treated as "abusive." I reasoned that their personal histories, perceptions, and opinions would lead to an increased understanding of child maltreatment and, perhaps, the identification of ways to address the problem. In addition to parents, I included staff members in the study. My intent was to access multiple sources of information, portray the problem from multiple perspectives, and, I hoped, thus develop a balanced representation of the problem.

My selection of this approach was influenced by Lightfoot's qualitative study on the emergence of school culture, *The Good High School* (1983), in which she described her research as based on the belief that:

> Environments and processes should be examined from the outsider's more distant perspective and the insider's immediate, subjective view; that the truth lies in the integration of various perspectives rather than in the choice of one as dominant and 'objective'; that one must always listen for the deviant voice as an important version of the truth (and as a useful indicator of what the culture or social group defines as normal), not disregard it as outside the central pattern (pp. 13–14).

Any portrayal of phenomena resulting from research is one of many possible versions depending upon what one chooses to ask, count, or observe. Although I gathered data from both parents and professionals, the views of parents predominate. I purposely sought and reported more of the parents' views than the staffs' views so that, as Goffman pointed out in *Asylums* (1961), the imbalance would, at least, be on the proper side of the scale.

The following description of the procedures I used to collect and analyze data should help clarify how the study was conducted. It is followed by a discussion of my relationships with the site and subjects. Within the context of the discussion, I made an effort to identify my biases about the parents, staff, and program.

A FIELD STUDY APPROACH

In order to access the outsider's distant perspective and the insider's immediate subjective view, I used a field study approach that included multiple methods of data collection. Zelditch (1962), in a classic article about naturalistic research, explained that a field study does not have to be conducted either quantitatively or qualitatively. Rather than being a single method of gathering a single kind of information, a field study approach incorporates three distinct strategies for obtaining three types of information: incidents and histories, distributions and frequencies, and generally known rules and statuses. Each type of information is most accurately and efficiently collected using certain methods: participant observations, interviews, and enumeration and sampling. (For a correlation of the type of information sought with the appropriate strategy, please see Table A.1.) The types of information and methods I used to collect each type of information are described in the following subsection.

Methods of obtaining information	Information types
Enumeration and samples	Frequency Distributions
Participant observations	Incidents, histories
Interviewing informants	institutionalized norms and statuses

Table A.1 *Types of information and corresponding methods of obtaining information using a field study approach*

Participant Observations

The first method I used to collect data was participant observation, the most complete and efficient strategy for gathering information about incidents and histories (Zelditch, 1962). Participant observations allowed data to be collected from their sources (families, staff members, and caseworkers) within the contexts in which events occurred (the program, homes, community). Participant observation is based on the premise that events are best understood by knowing and considering the settings in which they occur (Bogdan & Biklen, 1982). In practical terms, participant observations meant watching occurrences during particular times, in particular settings, then talking to the participants about what occurred and how they made sense of it. The exact setting, time, and incidents observed are at issue because although everything is grist for the qualitative mill, one cannot be everywhere and observe everything, and must observe something (Zelditch, 1962; Wolcott, 1989).

Because my interests centered around intervention for child maltreatment, and I am an educator interested in young children and their families, I began my observations in a place I thought would yield the information that would answer my questions—an intervention program for families. The intervention program proved to be a fertile starting place that generated many leads, although the study ended up being about many things in addition to intervention.

Participant observations typically lasted 5 hours, the duration of the intervention sessions from the time the staff arrived until they left. Observations and written recordings included staff meetings prior to intervention sessions, the arrival of parents and children to the program, intervention sessions with parents and children, debriefing sessions with parents, and staff meetings following intervention sessions. Seventeen observations were conducted in the parent program during the initial 4 months of the study. An additional 11 "observations" were conducted via phone with both parents and staff members over the subsequent 8 months. I describe these conversations as observations rather than interviews because they were unsolicited and unstructured, and were recorded in the form of field notes rather than verbatim transcriptions.

Initial observations in the intervention setting were relatively unfocused. They included descriptions of my entry into the research site— physical descriptions of the intervention setting, community, and participants, and intervention sessions. This excerpt from an initial observation reveals the general nature of the information I collected and the mild interest I generated from a parent during a time when parents were not yet willing to talk to me. My comments are enclosed in brackets.

> I was observing in Ellen's room. I ducked in to observe her circle time before lunch was served. Parents, children, and staff were sitting on the floor in a circle singing "Old MacDonald." . . . As the circle disperses for lunch, one of the parents asks an interventionist if she is the researcher, and the interventionist answers, "No." [The group is new so interventionists are also unknown to parents.] The parent says, "Well, she looks like you."

Later observations shifted from a focus on physical settings, classroom logistics, and descriptions of parents, children, and staff members to specific incidents experienced by families in the program. Observations in the program allowed me to become aware of important information about the families' lives not directly related to intervention. For example, I discovered that a toddler had broken his leg, his parents were reported to CPS by hospital staff, and their case was subsequently closed; that Jean and her sister brawled in an alley outside the program and several weeks later the same sister gave Jean's daughter a birthday party when Jean was out of money; that medical coupons would pay to have teeth pulled but not filled; that a caseworker interpreted the results of a parent's psychological examination with that parent although she lacked the expertise to do so and had no firsthand knowledge of the testing session; that Jean's daughter allegedly had been sexually abused in her foster care placement. Information flowed freely among staff members, among parents, and among staff members and parents.

The specific locations in which I happened to be observing influenced the content of my observations. However, noteworthy events were usual topics during staff planning and debriefing meetings, and sensitive information and opinions were shared with me by key informants—both staff and parents. I am certain I was not aware of all important events occurring in the lives of families, but events that emerged formed consistent patterns over time. Those events, and the questions they prompted, laid the foundation for the second method I used to collect information.

Interviews

Zelditch referred to the second kind of information included in a field study approach as "generally known rules and statuses." When I began this study I was already fairly well versed concerning what the experts had to say on the topic of child maltreatment. I wanted to know insiders' views of the problem. How did parents make sense of their involvement in CPS? What was generally understood about the child welfare system by parents who maltreated their children or staff who worked in the system? In order to access this information, I interviewed those closest to the problem — the parents and the staff. Rather than using my own words to describe observations in field notes, data were in the form of subjects' verbal descriptions of child maltreatment, the intervention program, CPS and their own lives and situations.

I conducted 18 interviews during the study. Following the study I collected two additional interviews, one with an individual parent and one with several staff members from the program, for the purpose of verifying the accuracy, plausibility, and authenticity of the study. Interviews typically lasted approximately 1½ hours during visits that ranged from 2½ to 5 hours in length. All interviews were audio-recorded. Interviews were open-ended to allow parents to lead conversations and tell me what was important to them. The interviews were in-depth to allow me to pursue areas I thought were important based on my initial analysis of data. The interviews permitted discovery of parents' personal histories related to their involvement with CPS and their views regarding their experiences (Taylor & Bogdan, 1984). Questions formed during the initial phase of the study when I began coding data collected during participant observations were embedded in later interviews to followup early leads.

Interviews allow access to multiple perspectives about single events or topics (Patton, 1980). For example, Ann told me that other parents in the program thought that the program was "stupid" and denied harming their children, yet parents I spoke to told me they thought CPS should have intervened in their families, and they made positive statements, such as Pauline's comment about the program, "It's kind of like a guiding light through a tunnel."

The interviews afforded access to past events, such as Ann's life history, and to the circumstances that lead to parents' initial involvement with CPS. They also allowed discovery of parents' thoughts and feelings such as Ann's reactions to her husband's drinking and violence and Pauline's fear during a visit from her caseworker. Although these events or types of information are not directly observable, they are critical to gaining an understanding of the physical and social contexts in which incidents of child maltreatment are embedded and the ways parents made sense of their involvement in the child welfare system.

Initial interviews included open-ended, relatively unstructured questions that would allow parents to identify and define issues from their perspectives (Merriam, 1988). For example, as we engaged in small talk about her children during our first interview, Jean stated that "when my kids got taken away it was like they took away my life. I never knew how valuable they were." I asked, "What was going on with you when all that happened?" Jean described specific incidents leading to her involvement with CPS, such as her visits to her boyfriend in jail, lack of suitable child care, and the sexual assault of her children by her brother.

Ann began describing her feelings about CPS during our first interview before I had an opportunity to start my tape recorder, so I began the taped interview with the following statement, "Ann was telling me about what happened when she first came into the program — what her feelings were." Ann responded with a question, "You want to know how I felt when I first came?" She then provided a detailed history of her initial involvement with CPS.

Although the initial interviews were general and exploratory, subsequent interviews incorporated specific questions about topics discussed earlier. The questions were recursive and became increasingly structured as data were analyzed and themes began to emerge. In addition to pursuing specific topics and issues, I used interview questions to verify hunches and confirm and clarify my understanding of the parents' statements and explanations. The situations that lead to families' involvement with CPS were so complicated, during the course of the study I asked similar questions numerous times or paraphrased what I believed parents told me in an attempt to make sense of what happened and make sure I understood their stories. The following excerpts from interviews with Ann cover the same topics at different times during the study. They illustrate the recursive nature of questions asked and the resulting clarification of information and insight into Ann's thoughts and feelings.

Interview with Ann, 5/18/89

Susan: The original report to CPS was from your mother-in-law?

Ann: And my doctor because I went to — because they wanted me to get on some medication. Tranquilizers or something, for my nerves.

Susan: Because you were feeling irritable?

Ann: I mean, you walked up behind me and I just jumped. I was shaking all the time, you know, and stuff like that.

Susan: Was it from just being off of drugs and alcohol? Do you think that's why you felt real irritable?

other state] and made me move here. He told me that I could either stay there in [the other state] and be by myself or come here
and be with my son. He threatened to take my son. Of course,
he says that's not the way it happened. But it is the way it happened. So I was mad about that. And I'm in a place where he
took me away from all my support, all my friends. And it was
just him drinking, threatening me all the time, and threatening
to take the baby. Then in my women's group in the mental
health clinic I was going to, I'd been going there 3 weeks before
this situation happened, and I said, "Look, I came here because
I was depressed and you guys aren't helping me." She told me if
I was depressed I ought to go read a book.

Susan: The mental health worker?

Ann: Yes. So I said, "I really need some help here because I'm just
afraid for me and my son." Well, she took that as I was threatening to hurt him, that I had threatened to hurt him. So they
turned me in and reported what I had said in group. I have had
no confidentiality. Everything I have told the mental health
worker went back to the CPS worker.

Interview with Ann, 7/11/89

Susan: I'm asking follow-up questions to Ann. This is the story I'm
telling about you. I want you to correct me if I'm wrong. You're
in another city and you're living with your mother-in-law. Both
you and Mike are living there with Ben.

Ann: At first.

Susan: Mike was drinking, and he left you with your mother-in-
law, left both you and Ben with your mother-in-law. You were
getting depressed and you went to a mental health group. You
went there for about 3 weeks before CPS got involved with you.

Ann: Yes. An important part is that I was asking for a psychologist a week before the incident happened, and I was put off.
That's very important.

Susan: What did they say when you asked?

Ann: She never returned my phone calls. She was never there,
and they just thought my problem was drugs and alcohol. I
tried to tell them it wasn't, and they would not let me have a
psychologist. All she was was just a drug and alcohol counselor.
They put me off. She was never there. They just wouldn't let me
have another counselor. That is a very important part right
there.

Susan: Tell me why you think it's important.

Ann: Because of the fact that I was trying to tell these people that I needed help . . . I mean, I hadn't even been drinking when the incident happened. And they were trying to tell me that all my problem was just drinking and drugs. And it wasn't.

Susan: Had you been using drugs?

Ann: No.

Susan: You were clean?

Ann: Yeah. That's the whole point. I was trying to tell them that I was suffering from depression and anxiety and all that, and they would not listen to me. And then the situation happened because I fell apart, and that's that. And that's a very important part, because if I had been able to see a psychologist, it might have not happened. See what I'm saying?

The redundancy of questions and topics allowed me to check the consistency of parents' stories as well as allowing me to confirm my understanding. By repeating questions and revisiting topics, I was able to detect novel information or information that did not fit the theories or explanations I developed. In this way I could determine if a topic was exhausted and data collection had reached a point of saturation.

Following the collection of participant observation and interview data, I collected data about the larger group of parents in the program. I postponed this data collection until the end of the study for two reasons. First, I wanted the parents' perspectives rather than the information from the questionnaires to direct the focus of the study. Second, I wanted the questionnaires to help me judge whether or not my beliefs about the problem based on the data collected from three families were consistent with those of the larger group.

Enumeration and Sampling

The third type of information presented in this study was collected by a survey, *The Family Information Questionnaire* (Veltman, Janko, & Sullivan, 1988 adapted by Janko & Firman, 1989). Enumeration and sampling data are useful in providing evidence of events that occurred previously (Zelditch, 1962). The survey used in this study provides demographic data about the subjects and history of their involvement in CPS in terms of child and family characteristics, patterns of service use, and outcomes of intervention.

The survey is one measure used by the program for monitoring program events, documenting characteristics of the families enrolled in the program, and evaluating program efficacy. The survey was used in this study to provide a multivariate description of families as a group. The individual families I observed and interviewed, rather than being viewed as typical or representative, should be viewed as presenting particular information that is important to know more about but difficult to discover by counting. Descriptive statistics produced by the survey allowed a synthesis of the outsider's perspective (we determined what to ask on the survey based on research and clinical opinion) and the insider's perspective (the parents decided what was important to tell me about child maltreatment).

Data for the survey were gathered for 55 parents and 97 children enrolled in the program during a 12-month period of time. Two staff members in the program completed the survey. One staff member was an author of the survey, and the other was a graduate student and employee of the Parenting Program who was responsible for collecting and compiling data for program evaluation. Both staff members knew the families through their work in the program, but had worked directly with only a few of the families. The forms were completed by program staff during an interview with CPS caseworkers who were managing the cases of families in the program.

Ten forms (18%) were checked for interobserver agreement using the following procedure. Both staff members simultaneously completed a survey while one staff member interviewed the caseworker. Items on the duplicate forms were compared item by item for agreement, and the number of items that were in agreement were divided by the total number of items on the survey (Kazdin, 1982). Interscorer agreement ranged from 88% to 100% with a mean of 97%. Data collected through participant observations and interviews were analyzed using a grounded theory approach, which is described in the following section.

A GROUNDED THEORY APPROACH

The grounded theory approach to qualitative research, articulated by Glaser and Strauss in 1967, is used to discover information and develop theories in contrast to quantitative methodologies that rely on preexisting theoretical frameworks (Charmaz, 1983). Four distinct strategies were identified by Charmaz as constituting the grounded theory approach and were used in this study for data collection and analysis.

First, data collection and analysis proceed simultaneously. From the first day data were collected for this study, analysis began. Each day following participant observations, I transcribed handwritten field notes and printed a paper copy for line-by-line coding. During the initial stages of coding, one searches for leads, ideas, and issues in each line of data. The data appear at first to be "a mass of confusing, unrelated accounts," but by studying the data and assigning labels to each line, the researcher begins to create order (Charmaz, 1983, p. 114).

During the initial stages of my study, I was unsure what to make of a frequently appearing label, "dental problems," which I had assigned to incidents of parents and children without teeth, parents with abscessed teeth or toothaches, and parents who could not afford dental care. This was clearly not what I expected to discover in the intervention setting and did not appear to have much to do with child maltreatment. As the study progressed, however, it became clear that medical and dental care were unaffordable luxuries to families in the program. Lack of available treatment resulted in recurrent pain and stress and were part of a larger pattern of families' inability to meet their basic needs for food, housing, transportation, and health care.

The second strategy identified by Charmaz was to structure the process of inquiry based on discoveries made during analysis. As labels reappear and relate to other labels, categories are developed and coding becomes more focused. Categories and subcategories can be created from the language of participants or developed according to the researcher's interests. For example, in Chapter 3 of this study, "Child Protective Services — Prevention and Intervention," I used the parents' own words to describe their initial involvement with CPS. As I described their situations, it seemed that the gist of what they were telling me was that their family situations were extremely complex when CPS investigated, that abuse and neglect were difficult to identify and define, and that CPS focused their intervention on one person in situations that involved many people.

The categories I created, substantiating abuse and legal intervention, included information that made me aware of those patterns, stimulated questions about the contexts of child maltreatment, and prompted me to question how intervention addressed the situations that initially resulted in CPS intervention and the ways in which parents got out of the system. These categories became subheadings in subsequent chapters.

The third strategy Charmaz described was the process of analysis that prompts discovery and theory development. As these larger categories and subcategories were developed and questions about them plagued me, I began to develop theories about families and child maltreatment. For example, one theory was that parents must appear motivated and earnest to caseworkers as a prerequisite to case closure. Program co-director Georgia talked about compliant parents as "the ones who get the results, regardless of what they can demonstrate with their children." An observation I made, one that now seems so obvious that I hesitate to describe it as a discovery, is that the duration of services have little to do with the scope of the problems and are not sufficient for making real changes in the lives of families; instead they appear to have more to do with funding and legal requirements. I suppose I had an awareness of the discrepancy between the importance and enormity of the problem and the brevity of the cure, but until I gathered information about many aspects of families' lives beyond those I was aware of as a program provider, and until I gathered information over an extended period of time, I do not think I realized how mismatched the problems and treatments were.

The fourth and final strategy described by Charmaz is that conceptual categories that emerge during analysis are refined, elaborated, and exhausted by a process of theoretical sampling. Many of the categories that emerged in my data were so obvious, common, and recurrent that I scarcely needed to make arrangements to collect additional samples to test my theories and discoveries. Families lived in poverty, in housing that was nonexistent or substandard, and lacked sources of social support. But more subtle points required talking to a number of people and looking deeper.

I came to believe that Ann relied on social service agencies from an early age and began to see them as family. I presented this theory to her during a particularly painful conversation. Her silence and tears made me think that my theory had some validity. She thought about what I had said for several minutes, then told me she hadn't thought of it like that, but that she believed it was true. This theory did not apply to all of the parents in the program, however. Despite professing a close relationship and affection for her CPS caseworkers, Jean came to the program only until her children were returned. The program, CPS, and the children's public school teachers did not hear of Jean again. Pauline came back for support during a time when she was having problems with Cody's behavior, but she began building relationships outside CPS and the program.

In addition to the four major strategies consistent with a grounded theory approach to qualitative research, I took steps to assure that my research would be complete, credible, dependable and straightforward. My efforts in that regard are described in the next section.

QUALITY ASSURANCE IN QUALITATIVE RESEARCH

Harry Wolcott (1990a), in a paper about validity in qualitative research, included the following quote from Clifford Geertz's essay "Thick Description":

> Cultural analysis is intrinsically incomplete and, worse than that, the more deeply it goes the less complete it is. It is a strange science whose most telling assertions are its most tremulously based, on which to get somewhere with the matter at hand is to intensify the suspicion, both your own and that of others, that you are not quite getting it right (p. 29).

Wolcott points out, however, that he takes considerable pains when conducting field studies "not to get it all wrong." He proceeds in the paper, and in the book he wrote subsequently, to describe the steps he takes to attempt to satisfy the challenge of conducting a "valid" field study (Wolcott, 1990b).

The first strategy described by Wolcott was that of being an attentive and responsive listener. Attempting to be a good listener while conducting this study, I conscientiously avoided asking leading questions and refrained from commenting on what was said. I was amazed at the quantity of information I gleaned when I asked so few questions. (Eventually I determined that the fewer questions I asked during interviews, the more I seemed to learn.) I was not always successful in refraining from comment, and at times was more a reactive than a responsive listener. Near the end of the study, when I was anxious to shed the role of researcher, Ann disclosed that she had struck her son, and I pleaded, "Oh, Ann, don't hit your son." A review of interview transcripts convinced me that my indiscretions were infrequent and that I recognized and remedied them during the course of the interviews in which they occurred.

As I listened during interviews and observations I encountered stories that seemed suspect or particularly important. Not wanting to appear too eager, I feigned ignorance so that the subjects would provide explanations or details. The parents omitted information when talking to me, but I did not detect outright falsehoods. They, especially the parent I called Jean, wanted to please me, I think, and told me things that might put them in a flattering light. (Jean told me how clean she always kept her children, although visual and olfactory inspection of them suggested otherwise.)

The second tactic Wolcott described was accurate recording of what people did and said. The record should be in the form of the subject's own words, when possible, and should occur during observations or interviews. I observed directly within situations and used 8½ " × 11" sheets of paper to record my field notes. I folded, numbered, and slipped the notes in my pocket after recording. (The sheets were relatively unobtrusive, at least to one who was trained as a behavioral scientist in systematic observation using clipboards that beeped intermittently to signal recording intervals.) When people seemed curious or apprehensive, I offered to let them look at my notes, but no one took advantage of my offer. I always transcribed my stacks of folded notes at the end of the same day they were recorded so that my memory would be fresh and I could avoid reinterpreting what I had observed.

Researchers are supposed to defer judgment and allow their data to tell the story when using a qualitative approach (Peshkin, 1985). However, even if judgments are delayed, researchers have hunches, or preconceptions, when they begin. The hunch shapes the research in certain ways (selection of subjects, locations, questions, methods) and is itself reshaped or transformed during the research process.

The third strategy I borrowed from Wolcott was that of writing at the beginning of the research for the purpose of recording what I already knew or suspected and identifying gaps in my information — prestating my hunches. My dissertation proposal served these purposes to some extent. For example, I listed the following questions as things I anticipated learning by the end of the study:

1. Do parents know why they are labeled?
2. What meaning do the labels have to parents and to service providers?
3. What is the parents' understanding of the reasons that they are receiving services?
4. What is the service providers' understanding of the reasons that parents, children, and/or families are receiving services?
5. Do parents think intervention is helpful, and in what ways?
6. Do service providers think intervention is helpful, and in what ways?
7. Are there aspects of intervention that are appealing to parents and children?
8. What are the obstacles to successful intervention from the point of view of parents and of service providers?
9. What are the reasons that parents give for wanting to maintain or re-establish custody of their children?
10. What are the motives that service providers assign to parents for wanting to maintain or re-establish custody of their children?

I wrote in my proposal that "the answers to these questions, and other questions and areas of interest consistent with the purpose of this study, should provide information about the perceptions of parents and interventionists that are enlightening and useful to professionals who provide services to maltreated children and their families." It should be apparent at this point that some of my preconceived notions at the outset of the study were different from what I came to discover — not surprising, since this is a primary advantage of a qualitative approach. Many of the questions I formed early on are unanswered and did not arise as issues or areas of great interest or importance to parents during the course of the study.

I also devoted attention in my proposal to describing the impact of child maltreatment on the development of children, yet, during the study, children were mentioned almost exclusively in the context of conversations about child custody. Development was rarely mentioned, with the exception of several anecdotes provided by parents when they expressed pride in their children's achievements. I thought developmental sequelae were important, and still do, but I do not think it was acknowledged as important by the subjects in this study. If the welfare system exists for the benefit of children who are maltreated, why was there so little attention to how the children fared once they entered the system? There is a notable difference between the academic literature that emphasizes the impact of maltreatment on children's social, emotional, cognitive, and behavioral development and the parents and CPS staff who failed to emphasize in words and actions concern about those aspects of child development and well-being.

Wolcott encourages inclusion of primary data in final accounts to give readers an idea of what the data are like. I used this tactic liberally. The data had such a powerful effect on me, I frequently was tempted to lift pages of interviews and insert them in my chapters. Access to whole interviews could be advantageous both in preserving the integrity of the data and allowing the reader to have sufficient information to allow criticism of my interpretations; however, this approach would probably significantly limit the number of people who would voluntarily read my study. I included as much primary data as I thought my audience would tolerate, and emphasized description rather than analysis or theory building.

Including primary data as much as possible also addresses the real problems that arise when one uses multiple sources, multiple methods, and triangulation to check developing theories. Wolcott notes that "anyone who has done fieldwork knows that if you address a question of any consequence to two or more informants you may as well prepare yourself for two different answers" (Wolcott, 1990b, p. 43). I tried to present the variety of answers I encountered and not to delimit the study to the narrow topics on which everyone saw things in approximately the same way.

Wolcott declared that he is not disconcerted when data do not fit his developing accounts or interpretations. As a fifth strategy, he includes his comments and observations of discrepant data in his accounts. I confess that I was greatly distressed throughout the study when things did not fit. I finally concluded that the more dissonance I felt, the better, because it meant that I was on to something—that this was something worth looking into. By no means did I figure out the answers to the questions I considered important. One benefit of the research to me personally was that it prompted me to ask questions I might never have asked if I hadn't conducted this study. I attempted to clearly indicate the points that I thought were important but that did not fit into my sense of what had occurred.

Because Wolcott believes that subjectivity is a strength of qualitative research, he includes personal feelings and reactions in his accounts to the extent that they seem relevant. This strategy appears to have merit because it allows readers to identify the author's position and biases. At the same time, it strikes me as threatening to the integrity of the research if the account becomes more about the researcher's reactions to the subject than an accurate description of it.

Wolcott draws a distinction between revealing feelings and imposing judgments and explains that one is research and the other reform. I was concerned about my ability to make this distinction during this study. My interest in conducting the study stemmed from my dissatisfaction with the intervention approaches used in the child welfare system. Throughout the study I struggled to keep my previous role of program developer from taking precedence. I wanted to know what worked and what did not. Chapter 6, "Getting Out of the System," grew from my desire to identify which interventions were effective in making parents "good parents." The study did not answer my questions about intervention because that was not what the study was about, so I went to consumers to see if they had any ideas. It was unsettling to me not to have answers. In the dissertation I attempted to hold this tendency in check by carefully reviewing the study, and identifying judgments, then deleting them or labeling them as such. I focused on describing what parents and staff thought worked and what did not to refrain from prescribing what should be done. In this book, I built a bridge—one that is much needed, in my opinion—from research to reform. My opinions and feelings should be evident.

As a seventh strategy to try to keep from getting the story wrong, Wolcott suggests sharing developing manuscripts with informed readers. Doctoral dissertations are an asset in this regard because they provide the researcher with a captive audience. Dianne Ferguson's reviews were invaluable, as were our subsequent conversations. She detected value judgments, asked questions that forced me to consider alternative views, and encouraged me to verbalize stories and impose structure and order on a developing mass of confusing categories.

Toward the end of the study, I shared the manuscripts with a colleague in the intervention site to check accuracy, completeness, and authenticity. I also shared the manuscripts with novices and, following their readings, asked them what they got from the chapters and if they got it in a way that was clear and understandable.

Wolcott's eighth strategy is a return to the field setting or a rereading of field notes from start to finish — a chore he describes as onerous. I liked rereading my field notes because it allowed me to work on my study while simultaneously avoiding the more onerous task of writing. It was also a valuable method of checking the accuracy of my accounts. Despite a researcher's best efforts, memories are fallible and important details may be overlooked. I thus sat with field notes on one side and manuscript on the other and verified events or revised accounts when my field notes and manuscript were not in accord.

As a parallel activity, Wolcott reads his manuscripts with an eye focused on technical accuracy. I performed this task months after I wrote most of the chapters of this book, when I had been long enough away to see my words with a fresh view. This check for coherence and internal consistency seemed especially pertinent because this study was conducted and written over a 2-year period. During that time not only my reactions but also the parents' situations changed. I wanted to make sure that my account was true to the original data but also that it was presented in a cogent manner, one that reflected how I finally made sense of things rather than documenting my confusion along the way.

These strategies employed during data collection and analysis did, I hope, add to the trustworthiness, clarity, and cogency of this study. A remaining issue related to the quality of qualitative research is the role of the researcher; and, in this study, my role as a researcher in a program where I was also known as a friend and colleague.

ADOPTING THE ROLE OF RESEARCHER

Just as a tool that purports to measure some object or construct requires certain qualities (internal consistency, evidence of its reliability, cultural sensitivity), a researcher who purports to account for some phenomenon requires certain prerequisites to obtain sufficient and quality data. Some prerequisites that are frequently mentioned include rapport and trust with informants (Taylor & Bogdan, 1984), participation in activities (Van Maanen, 1983), learning the language of your subjects (Spradley, 1980), and finding key informants (Bogdan & Biklen, 1982; Taylor & Bogdan, 1984). Less frequently mentioned, perhaps because it is so difficult to discuss and so personally sensitive for the researcher, is the issue of personal relationships with research subjects.

In my introductory chapter, I stated that I was at one time a director of the program in which I conducted this study. I knew and worked with many of the people who staffed the program during my study. While I directed the program I wrote a federal demonstration grant that funded a portion of the program, and in conjunction with that grant and following this study, a colleague and I wrote a curriculum describing the intervention approach.

The benefit of this history was that I was well-known to staff, and, I believe, was trusted and respected by them. My entry into the system was expedited, and most staff members were willing informants throughout the study. (Aides who worked for CPS were the exception and did not provide information.) I was familiar with and comfortable in the program and began collecting data that were rich in detail and issues relatively early in the study. At the same time, my familiarity with the program, and my accustomed ways of understanding it, no doubt screened events I might otherwise have noticed and thus influenced my interpretations.

In an attempt to address any concerns that might stem from this observation, I will point out that my study ended up having less to do with the program per se than with the contexts of child maltreatment and the child welfare system as a whole. An antidote to this potential problem came as a result of the time I invested in the study beyond the time I spent collecting data. As of this writing, I began collecting data in the program 14 months ago and collected data on site for 14 weeks. During the remaining 11 months of the study, data were collected outside the program from parents who were no longer involved or minimally involved with the program.

My contacts with many staff members, and especially with one of the directors, Georgia, continues to the present. They keep me apprised of events that concern the families in my study. Although I never divulged the identities of the families that participated in the study, the families were not at all reluctant to share that information with program staff. Jean referred to me at one time as her "best friend" during a conversation with a staff member, and after I moved from the city in which the study occurred, Ann made a point of stopping in the program office to tell staff she spent time with me each time I visited the area. (Staff reported feeling annoyed that I hadn't visited them, and they thought Ann came in to gloat.)

My pre-existing relationships with staff seemed to me to be an asset after my role was firmly established and staff ceased asking my advice or opinion. This excerpt from my field notes is about how I broached this subject with staff.

> The meeting started with introductions of the participants of the meeting by the program director. Each person introduced themselves in turn. When it came my turn, I said that I was, as of today, officially a data collector. Someone asked me if I was still supervising students, and I said not for any of the families I observed and mostly for procedural issues such as developing goal attainment scales. I clarified that if my junior student had questions or issues, that she was going to solicit help from my senior student. Someone else asked me if I would participate in Debrief. I said that if I did, it would be as an observer. I added that I would no longer give my opinions. That stimulated some hoots and laughter and comments that "that would be hard."

A shift in the way I was viewed by staff occurred several weeks into the study, according to my field notes, and staff stopped soliciting my opinions. They also began taking me aside or phoning me at home to relay information that had not been discussed during staff meetings.

The relationships that proved most difficult were those with the people who I had not known previously—the families. Relationships influenced who participated in the study. One parent who consented to participate had a boyfriend who was feared because of his reputation for being violent. I did not include her in the study because I was unwilling to take the chance of going to their home alone or writing something that might incite his anger at a later time. Recently, Georgia provided an update on the families in the study, and none were faring well. She commented that many families really did do well after intervention. She hypothesized that perhaps the families who were willing to talk to me were exceptionally needy, and wanted support. I think there is some merit in Georgia's analysis of the situation, but it is also possible that we do not really know how families fare after the program because we do not follow them or scrutinize their lives to the extent that I did during this research. I do agree that the relationships I was able to establish influenced which people participated in the study and determined which stories I discovered. I also believe that one story is as valuable as the next.

Johnson, in his 1975 essay on trust and personal involvement in fieldwork, described how observers' feelings become fused with their accounts. He described the anxiety he felt when his research began and his naive belief that trust would develop to a point where it would operate independently of the daily flux. Instead, he found that relationships were an inherent part of the daily flux.

In this study, my relationships with all of my subjects took ongoing efforts to maintain. I found it necessary to assure subjects throughout the study that their participation was voluntary, their statements were confidential, and I did not discuss our conversations with others. Ann intermittently checked to make sure her husband's identity was protected, asking, "You're not using his real name, are you?" One evening I delivered half of my husband's birthday cake to her house, and he accompanied me because Ann lived in an unsafe neighborhood. I asked him to wait in the car as I took it to her door, and she expressed interest in meeting him. She commented that he probably knew all about her, and I reassured her that I did not talk about the families in my study or use their real names.

A second issue Johnson discussed concerning relationships while conducting research is the personal reactions the researcher has to situations discovered during research. Research on child maltreatment provided fertile ground for reacting. The homes I visited were at times uncomfortable for me because some were filthy, impoverished, or in dangerous neighborhoods. Some associates of the parents made me feel apprehensive and frightened, and some events were alien to me and personally repulsive. Other events struck a most personal chord. I allowed myself to be open with the parents to a greater extent than I typically am with friends or colleagues so that I might reciprocate their generosity in sharing the most personal parts of their lives. One evening as I transcribed a taped interview I had conducted with Jean, I heard her talk about the sexual abuse she had experienced as a child and I heard my voice affirming that it was painful, that I too had been sexually abused as a child. This fact, never having been shared before and now publicly stated, created a personal dilemma for me.

Did these reactions compromise the research? They did influence it. I limited the interviews to a number I thought I could manage, not only physically and logistically but also emotionally. I interpreted data and directed questions with an eye toward identifying remedies to problems in an effort to counterbalance frequent feelings of demoralization, helplessness, and profound sadness. I organized the book by incorporating the parents' and staff's hopes that the reasons families were involved with the child welfare system would someday cease to exist, and the system's response to other families would occur earlier and be more effective.

A third issue was related to the ongoing and changeable nature of personal relationships. My relationship with Ann has been the most problematic for me. I was, one staff member told me, "the most important person in her life." I hope that was not true, but I acknowledge an awareness of being more important to Ann than I felt comfortable being. As I have stated, I believe that people from agencies have replaced Ann's family and friends as her social support. I found myself in that role as well, and during the study I regularly accepted collect phone calls despite living on a very limited budget myself, and visited Ann when I didn't take time to visit others I might have preferred to visit.

Part of my behavior was the result of a genuine fondness for Ann and sincere wish to listen when she needed to talk. She always thanked me for listening and I always responded by thanking her in turn for sharing so openly because I learned a lot that was helpful to my research. I attempted to make her feel valued while reminding her that I was conducting research. I also took pains not to offend her, or any of the other parents, because I realized the tentativeness of their relationships with agencies, and I worried that they would withdraw consent and undermine my research. I walked a fine line at times trying to accommodate the parents so that they would accommodate me, while exercising caution so as not to exploit their trust and generosity.

Did my personal relationships with the staff and parents compromise my research? I think they allowed me to discover things I would not have discovered as a detached observer. They also increased the likelihood that what I discovered was truthful and accurate (Johnson, 1975). The multiple data sources resulting from the number of relationships I established allowed easy confirmation of events—almost automatic triangulation. Most importantly, and the bottom line with fieldwork, is that without the benefit of personal relationships, regardless of the hazards, these families' stories would go untold.

REFERENCES

Adler, J., Beachy, L., Seligman, J., Rogers, P., Azar, V., McGinn, D., & Gordon, J. (1992, August 31). Unhappily ever after. *Newsweek*, pp. 52–59.

Agar, M. (1980). *The professional stranger: An informal introduction to ethnography*. Orlando, FL: Academic Press.

Alsop, R. (1990, April). *News release: Data on child abuse and neglect*. Denver, CO: American Humane Association.

American Humane Association. (1986). *Highlights of official child neglect and abuse reporting*. Denver, CO: Author.

Anastasi, A. (1976). *Psychological testing* (4th ed.). New York: MacMillan.

Anastasiow, N. (1986). The research base for early intervention. *Journal of the Division of Early Childhood, 10*(2), 99–105.

Annie E. Casey Foundation. (1992). *Kids count data book*. Washington, DC: Center for the Study of Social Policy.

Auletta, K. (1983). *The underclass*. New York: Vintage Books.

Barden, J. C. (1991, January 6). Foster care kids over-represented among homeless. *The Seattle Times/Seattle Post Intelligencer*, p. A13.

Bellah, R. N., Madsen, R., Sullivan, W. M., Swidler, A., & Tipton, S. M. (1985). *Habits of the heart*. Berkeley: University of California Press.

Belsky, J. (1980). Child maltreatment: An ecological integration. *American Psychologist, 35*, 430–435.

Belsky, J., & Vondra, J. (1989). Lessons from child abuse: The determinants of parenting. In D. Cichetti & V. Carlson (Eds.), *Child maltreatment: Theory and research on the causes and consequences of child abuse and neglect* (pp. 153–202). Cambridge, England: Press Syndicate of the University of Cambridge.

Bijou, S. (1966). Theory and research in mental (developmental) retardation. *Psychological Record, 13*, 95–110.

Bogdan, R., & Biklen, S. (1982). *Qualitative research for education: An introduction to methods and theories*. Boston: Allyn & Bacon.

Bowman, B. (1992). Who is at risk for what and why? *Journal of Early Intervention, 16*(2), 101–108.

Bronfenbrenner, U. (1977). Toward an experimental ecology of human development. *American Psychologist, 32*, 513–531.

Bronfenbrenner, U. (1979). *The ecology of human development: Experiments of nature and design*. Cambridge, MA: Harvard University Press.

Charmaz, K. (1983). The grounded theory method: An explication and interpretation. In R. M. Emerson (Ed.), *Contemporary field research* (pp. 109–126). Boston: Little, Brown.

Children's Defense Fund. (1990). *A children's defense budget.* Washington, DC: Author.

Cicchetti, D., & Carlson, V. (1989). *Child maltreatment: Theory and research on the causes and consequences of child abuse and neglect.* Cambridge, England: Press Syndicate of the University of Cambridge.

Cicchetti, D., & Rizley, R. (1981). Developmental perspectives on the etiology, intergenerational transmission, and sequelae of child maltreatment. In R. Rizley & D. Cichetti (Eds.), *Developmental perspectives on child maltreatment: New directions for child development* (Vol. 2, pp. 78–103). San Francisco: Jossey-Bass.

Cornell Empowerment Project. (Undated). *Empowerment through family support.* Ithaca, NY: Cornell University Press.

Dorris, M. (1989). *The broken cord.* New York: Harper & Row.

Dubowitz, H. (1986). *Child maltreatment in the United States: Etiology, impact and prevention.* Background paper prepared for the Congress of the United States, Office of Technology Assessment, Washington, DC.

Edgar, E. (1988). Policy factors influencing research in early childhood special education. In S. L. Odom & M. B. Karnes (Eds.), *Early intervention for infants and children with handicaps.* Baltimore, MD: Paul H. Brookes.

Edgar, E. (1991, November). *Social justice and the search for equity for persons with disabilities.* Paper presented to the Office of Special Education Program Project Director's meeting, Washington, DC.

Egeland, B. (1988). Breaking the cycle of abuse: Implications for prediction and intervention. In K. D. Browne, C. Davies, & P. Stratton (Eds.), *Early prediction and prevention of child abuse.* New York: J. Wiley & Sons.

Egeland, B., & Erickson, M. F. (1987). Psychologically unavailable caregiving. In M. Brussard, B. Germain, & S. Hart (Eds.), *Psychological maltreatment of children and youth.* New York: Pergamon.

Egeland, B., & Erickson, M. F. (1990). Rising above the past: Strategies for helping new mothers break the cycle of abuse and neglect. *Zero to Three, 11*(2), 29–35.

Egeland, B., & Sroufe, L. (1981). Developmental sequelae of maltreatment in infancy. In R. Rizley & D. Cichetti (Eds.), *Developmental perspectives on child maltreatment: New directions for child development* (Vol. 2, pp. 104–132). San Francisco: Jossey-Bass.

Egeland, B., Sroufe, L., & Erickson, M. F. (1983). Developmental consequences of different patterns of maltreatment. *Child Abuse and Neglect, 7*(4), 459–469.

Elmer, E. (1977). *Fragile families, troubled children.* Pittsburgh, PA: University of Pittsburgh Press.

Erickson, M., Egeland, B., Musick, J., & Olds, D. (1991). *What, when, why, where, and how? Shaping the next generation of prevention research with families at risk.* Symposium conducted at the biannual meeting of the Society for Research in Child Development, Seattle, WA.

Erickson, M., Egeland, B., & Pianta, R. (1989). Effects of maltreatment on the development of young children. In D. Cichetti & V. Carlson (Eds.), *Child maltreatment: Theory and research on the causes and consequences of child abuse and neglect* (pp. 647–684). Cambridge, England: Press Syndicate of the University of Cambridge.

Fanshel, D., & Shinn, E. (1978). *Children in foster care: A longitudinal investigation.* New York: Columbia University Press.

Frost, R. (1969). *The poetry of Robert Frost.* New York: Holt, Rinehart & Winston.

Garbarino, J. (1976). A preliminary study of some ecological correlates of child abuse: The impact of socioeconomic status on the mother. *Child Development, 47,* 178–185.

Garbarino, J. (1988). *The future as if it really mattered.* Longmont, CO: Bookmakers Guild.

Garbarino, J. (1990). The human ecology of early risk. In S. J. Meisels & J. P. Shonkoff (Eds.), *Handbook of early childhood intervention* (pp. 78–96). New York: Cambridge University Press.

Gelles, R. (1979). *Family violence.* Beverly Hills, CA: Sage Publications.

Gil, D. (1970). *Violence against children: Physical abuse in the United States.* Cambridge, MA: Harvard University Press.

Giovannoni, J. (1989). Definitional issues in child maltreatment. In D. Cichetti & V. Carlson (Eds.), *Child maltreatment: Theory and research on the causes and consequences of child abuse and neglect* (pp. 3–37). Cambridge, England: Press Syndicate of the University of Cambridge.

Glaser, B., & Strauss, A. (1967). *The discovery of grounded theory: Strategies for qualitative research.* Chicago: Aldine.

Goffman, E. (1961). *Asylums.* Garden City, NY: Doubleday.

Gross, R., Speiker, D., Casey, P., Brooks-Gunn, J., & Ramey, C. (1990, April). The Infant Health and Development Program (IHDP) for low birth weight, premature infants. *Infant Behavior & Development: Abstracts of Papers Presented at the Seventh International Conference on Infant Studies* (pp. 96–97). Montreal.

Horowitz, B., & Wolock, I. (1981). Maternal deprivation, child maltreatment, and agency intervention. In L. H. Pelton (Ed.), *The social context of child abuse and neglect* (pp. 157–189). New York: Human Services Press.

Janko, S., & Firman, C. (1989). *Revised Family Information Questionnaire.* Eugene, OR: Center on Human Development, University of Oregon. (Adapted from M. Veltman, S. Janko, & K. Sullivan, *Family Information Questionnaire.* [1988])

Johnson, J. M. (1975). *Doing field research.* New York: Free Press.

Kaufman, J., & Zigler, E. (1989). The intergenerational transmission of child abuse. In D. Cichetti & V. Carlson (Eds.), *Child maltreatment: Theory and research on the causes and consequences of child abuse and neglect* (pp. 129–152). Cambridge, England: Press Syndicate of the University of Cambridge.

Kazdin, A. E. (1982). *Single-case research designs.* New York: Oxford University Press.

Kelly, W. (1992). *Pogo* cartoon. In J. Kaplan (Ed.), *Familiar quotations*. Boston: Little, Brown.

Kempe, C. H., & Helfer, R. (1972). *Helping the battered child and his family*. Philadelphia: J. B. Lippincott.

Kempe, C. H., Silverman, F., Steele, B., Droegemueller, W., & Silver, H. K. (1962). The battered child syndrome. *Journal of the American Medical Association, 181,* 4–11.

Kempe, R., & Kempe, C. H. (1978). *Child abuse*. Cambridge, MA: Harvard University Press.

Kozol, J. (1988). *Rachel and her children*. New York: Fawcett Columbine.

Kuhn, T. (1970). *The structure of scientific revolutions*. Chicago, IL: University of Chicago Press.

Lightfoot, S. H. (1983). *The good high school*. New York: Basic Books.

Lutzger, J. R., Frame, R. E., & Rice, J. M. (1982). Project 12-Ways: An ecobehavioral approach to the treatment and prevention of child abuse and neglect. *Education and Treatment of Children, 5,* 141–155.

Main, M., & Goldwyn, R. (1984). Predicting rejection of her infant from mother's representation of her own experience: Implication for the abused-abusing intergenerational cycle. *Child Abuse and Neglect, 8,* 203–217.

Mayor's Task Force on Child Abuse and Neglect. (1983, November 21). *Report on the preliminary study of child fatalities*. New York.

Meier, J. H. (1978). *A multifactorial model of child abuse dynamics* (Monograph No. 3:4/83). Beaumont, CA: Research Division, CHILDHELP U.S.A./INTERNATIONAL.

Meier, J. H., & Sloan, M. P. (1984). The severely handicapped child and child abuse. In J. Blacher (Ed.), *Severely handicapped young children and their families* (pp. 247–272). Orlando, FL: Academic Press.

Merriam , S. (1988). *Case study research in education: A qualitative approach*. San Francisco: Jossey-Bass.

Miller, A. (1987). *Maternal health and infant survival*. Washington, DC: National Center for Clinical Infant Programs.

Minuchin, S. (1974). *Families and family therapy*. Cambridge, MA: Harvard University Press.

Minuchin, S. (1991, Spring). Family abuse and neglect . . . Child welfare system indicted. *The Prevention Report* (pp. 7–8). Oakdale, IA: The National Resource Center on Family Based Services.

Moynihan, D. P. (1993). Defining deviancy down. *American Scholar, 62*(1), 17–30.

Newberger, C. M., & Cook, S. (1983). Parental awareness and child abuse: A cognitive-developmental analysis of urban and rural samples. *American Journal of Orthopsychiatry, 53,* 512–524.

Offord, D. R. (1982). Primary prevention: Aspects of program design and evaluation. *Journal of American Academy of Child Psychiatry, 21*(1), 225–230.

Olds, G., & Henderson, C. R. (1989). The prevention of maltreatment. In D. Cichetti & V. Carlson (Eds.), *Child maltreatment: Theory and research on the causes and consequences of child abuse and neglect* (pp. 3–37). Cambridge, England: Press Syndicate of the University of Cambridge.

Orwell, G. (1946). *Animal farm*. New York: Harcourt Brace Jovanovich.

Palfrey, J., Singer, J., Walker, D., & Butler, J. (1987). Early identification of children's special needs: A study in five metropolitan communities. *Journal of Pediatrics, 11*, 651–659.

Patton, M. Q. (1980). *Qualitative evaluation methods*. Newbury Park, CA: Sage Publications.

Pelton, L. H. (1978). Child abuse and neglect: The myth of classlessness. *American Journal of Orthopsychiatry, 48*, 608–617.

Pelton, L. H. (1985). *The social context of child abuse and neglect*. New York: Human Sciences Press.

Pelton, L. H. (1989). *For reasons of poverty: A critical analysis of the public child welfare system in the United States*. New York, NY: Praeger.

Pelton, L. H. (Fall, 1990). Resolving the crisis in child welfare. *Public Welfare, 11*, 21–25.

Peshkin, A. (1985). From title to title: The evolution of perspective in naturalistic inquiry. *Anthropology and Education Quarterly, 16*, 214–223.

Pianta, R. (1990). Widening the debate on educational reform: Prevention as a viable alternative. *Exceptional Children, 56*(4), 306–313.

Pianta, R., Egeland, B., & Erickson, M. F. (1989). The antecedents of maltreatment: results of the Mother-Child Interaction Research Project. In D. Cichetti & V. Carlson (Eds.), *Child maltreatment: Theory and research on the causes and consequences of child abuse and neglect* (pp. 203–253). Cambridge, England: Press Syndicate of the University of Cambridge.

Ramey, C., Bryant, D., Sparling, J., & Wasik, B. (1985). Project CARE: A comparison of two early intervention strategies to prevent retarded development. *Topics in Early Childhood Special Education, 5*, 12–25.

Ramey, C., & Campbell, F. (1984). Preventive education for high-risk children: Cognitive consequences of the Carolina Abecedarian Project. *American Journal of Mental Deficiency, 88*, 515–523.

Reiss, D. (1981). *The family's construction of reality*. Cambridge, MA: Harvard University Press.

Reiss, D. (1990). The represented and practicing family: Contrasting visions of family continuity. In A. J. Sameroff & R. N. Emde (Eds.), *Relationship disturbances in early childhood* (pp. 191–220). New York: Basic Books.

Rescorla, L., Provence, S., & Naylor, A. (1983). Yale Child Welfare Research Program: Description and results. In E. Zigler & E. Gordon (Eds.), *Day care: Scientific and social policy issues*. Boston: Auburn House.

Rutter, M. (1989). Intergenerational continuities and discontinuities in serious parenting difficulties. In D. Cichetti & V. Carlson (Eds.), *Child maltreatment: Theory and research on the causes and consequences of child abuse and neglect* (pp. 317–348). Cambridge, England, Cambridge.

Sameroff, A., & Chandler, M. (1975). Reproductive risk and the continuum of caretaking casualty. In F. Horowitz, M. Hetherington, S. Scarr-Salapatek, & G. Siegel (Eds.), *Review of child development research* (Vol. 4, pp. 187–244). Chicago: Society for Research in Child Development.

Schwendiman, M., & Porter, A. (1990, August 21). What's wrong with kids? Poverty, mainly. *Seattle Times*, p. A7.

Shapiro, I., & Greenstein, R. (1988). *Holes in the safety nets: Poverty programs and policies in the U.S., national overview*. Washington, DC: Center on Budget and Policy Priorities.

Sia, C. J., & Breakey, G. (1985). The role of the medical home in child abuse prevention and positive child development. *Hawaii Medical Journal, 44*(7), 242–243.

Simeonsson, R. (1991). Primary, secondary, and tertiary prevention in early intervention. *Journal of Early Intervention, 15*(2), 124–134.

Skinner, B. F. (1953). *Science and human behavior*. New York: Macmillan.

Skrtic, T. (1991). *Behind special education: A critical analysis of professional culture and school organization*. Denver: Love.

Smith, M., & Pazder, L. (1989). *Michelle remembers*. New York: Simon & Schuster.

Spradley, J. P. (1980). *Participant observation*. New York: Holt, Rinehart & Winston.

Strauss, M. A., & Gelles, R. J. (1986). Change in family violence from 1975–1985. *Journal of Marriage and the Family, 48*, 465–479.

Suzuki, S. (1992). *Zen mind, beginner's mind*. New York: Weatherhill.

Taylor, S. J., & Bogdan, R. (1984). *Introduction to qualitative research methods: The search for meaning*. New York: John Wiley & Sons.

Tjossem, T. (1976). Early intervention: Issues and approaches. In T. Tjossem (Ed.), *Intervention strategies for high risk infants and young children* (p. 5). Baltimore: University Park Press.

Van Maanen, J. (1983). *Qualitative methodology*. Beverly Hills, CA: Sage Publications.

Wolcott, H. (1990a). On seeking — and rejecting — validity in qualitative research. In E. W. Eisner & A. Peshkin (Eds.), *Qualitative inquiry and education: The continuing debate* (pp. 121–152). New York: Teachers College Press.

Wolcott, H. (1990b). *Writing up qualitative research*. Beverly Hills, CA: Sage Publications.

Wolfe, D. (1985). Child abusive parents: An empirical review and analysis. *Psychological Bulletin, 97*, 462–482.

Woodward, J. K. (1991, June). The sins of the father. *Newsweek, 119*, 60–61.

Zelditch, M. (1962). Some methodological problems of field studies. *American Journal of Sociology, 67*, 566–576.

Zigler, E. (1990). Foreword. In S. J. Meisels & J. P. Shonkoff (Eds.), *Handbook of early intervention*. New York: Cambridge University Press.

Zigler, E., & Hall, N. (1989). Physical child abuse in America: Past, present, and future. In D. Cichetti & V. Carlson (Eds.), *Child maltreatment: Theory and research on the causes and consequences of child abuse and neglect* (pp. 38–75). Cambridge, England: Press Syndicate of the University of Cambridge.

INDEX

Adler, J., 1
Agar, M., 12
Alsop, R., 1
American Humane Association, 25
Anastasi, A., 80
Anastasiow, Nicholas, 121, 125, 135
Ann (parent), 73–74
  abused as child, 27
  and acquiring parenting skills, 97
  and changing system, 125–126, 135–136
  CPS and, 66, 70–71
  earnestness of, 106–107
  and empowering parents, 86, 88, 90–91
  family history of, 27–29, 52, 55
  and getting out of system, 105–117
  intervention and, 34–36, 98–99
  Parenting Program and, 47–49
  and perpetuation of child maltreatment,
    50, 52
  and preventing child maltreatment, 91
  professional relationships and, 77–78
  story of, 19–22
  study methods and, 141–144, 147–148,
    154–156
  substantiating child abuse and, 32–33
Annie E. Casey Foundation, 59
Auletta, K., 127

Barden, J. C., 65
Bellah, R. N., 121
Belsky, J., 2, 55
Bijou, S., 39
Biklen, S., 139, 153
Bogdan, R., 139, 141, 153
Bowman, Barbara, 2, 123, 125, 135
Breakey, G., 130
Bronfenbrenner, Uri, 25, 37–38, 120–121,
  123, 125
Brooks-Gunn, J., 133
Bryant, D., 133
Butler, J., 129

Campbell, F., 133
Carlson, V., 1
Carr, Mary, 125–127

Caseworkers
  and changing system, 119
  child's best interest and, 63
  CPS and, 66–71
  and getting out of system, 102, 106–107,
    114, 118
  intervention and, 33, 35, 99
  and parent and professional relation-
    ships, 76–86
  Parenting Program and, 38–40, 44
  poverty and, 56, 58
  study methods and, 139, 145, 147
Casey, P., 133
Chamberlain, 39
Chandler, Michael, 2, 39, 73
Charmaz, K., 145–147
Child abuse
  contribution of stress in precipitating,
    71–72
  definitions of, 4–7, 120, 126
  determinants of, 2–4
  intergenerational transmission of, 50,
    73, 115
  misperceptions of, 1–2, 30
  perpetuation of, 50–54
  prevalence of, 1–2, 4
  prevention of, 5, 37–42, 91–93, 130–132
  professionals' ability to recognize, 6
  social construction of, 4–7
  social significance of, 1–2
  substantiation of, 31–37
Child Protective Services (CPS), 29–49,
  66–74. See also Foster care and foster
  parents; Parenting Program
  adversarial relationship with, 70–71
  and changing system, 119–120, 125–
    126, 131
  children removed by, 15–17, 19, 21, 24–
    25, 29, 32–36, 66, 69, 77–79, 104–105
  child's best interest and, 61–63, 66
  and determinants of child abuse, 3
  and earnestness of parents, 106–108
  and empowering parents, 86, 88–89, 91
  family histories and, 25–26, 29–30

Child Protective Services (*continued*)
  functions of, 66–70
  and getting out of system, 101–104,
    106–108, 111–115, 117–118
  goals and purposes of, 8
  intervention and, 33–36, 98–100
  and parent and professional relation-
    ships, 75–79, 82–85
  parents and, 8, 66–73
  and perpetuation of child maltreatment,
    52, 54
  poverty and, 55–56, 61
  and preventing maltreatment, 91–93
  and providing parenting knowledge and
    skills, 93, 95
  service contracts of, 67–68, 81, 85, 103
  and social construction of child abuse, 7
  stories of parents involved with, 15–25
  study methods and, 9–13, 140–147, 150,
    153
  substantiating child abuse and, 32–33
Children
  and acquiring parenting skills and
    strengthening relationships with par-
    ents, 93–98
  acting in best interests of, 61–66
  and changing system, 123–127, 129–136
  characteristics of, 2–3, 10
  demographics of, 10
  developmental problems of, 80–81, 122,
    129–130
  honesty of, 16
  mentioned infrequently by parents and
    staff, 25–26
  Parenting Program and, 43–46
  in poverty, 12, 55–61
  removed by CPS, 15–17, 19, 21, 24–25,
    29, 32–36, 66, 69, 77–79, 104–105
  security for, 17–18
  study methods and, 140–142, 145–147,
    149–150
Children's Defense Fund, 59–60
Cichetti, D., 1, 55
Cook, S., 72
Cornell Empowerment Project, 119
Cowan, 73

Deal, 39
Dorris, M., 65–66
Droegemueller, W., 5
Dubowitz, H., 1
Dunst, 39

Edgar, E., 121, 129
Egeland, Byron, 2, 54, 56, 59, 72–73, 115,
  117, 119
Ellerbeck, Brian, 122–123
Elmer, E., 31, 60
Environment, 73
  as determinant in child abuse, 2–3
  family histories and, 25
  and getting out of system, 110–111
  Parenting Program and, 39, 42–44
  and perpetuation of child maltreatment,
    53
  poverty and, 58–59
  professionals' assessments of, 83–84
Erickson, M. F., 2, 56, 59, 73, 115, 117,
  119

Families. *See* Parents
Family histories
  of Ann, 27–29, 52, 55
  of Jean, 26–27, 50–52, 55
  of parents, 25–30, 50–52, 54–56, 59
  of Pauline, 29–30, 55–56
  poverty and, 56, 59
Family theory, 54–55
Fanshel, D., 65
Ferguson, Dianne, 152
Firman, C., 144
Foster care and foster parents, 8, 61–66,
  89, 104, 115
  for Ann's children, 19, 21, 29, 32–36
  and child's best interest, 61–65
  consequences of, 65
  factors in determining number of chil-
    dren in, 6
  for Jean's child, 51
  lack of, 63
  and legal intervention, 34–36
  maltreatment in, 62–64
  and Parenting Program, 38, 40, 44, 46
  for Pauline and her son, 22, 24–25, 34
  and preventing maltreatment, 93
  and social construction of child abuse,
    5–6
  time children spend in, 34
Frost, Robert, 14, 26

Garbarino, J., 4, 25, 56, 71, 73, 113
Gelles, R. J., 1, 6, 31
Georgia (program co-director)
  and changing system, 119
  child's best interest and, 63–65
  and empowering parents, 89–90

and getting out of system, 101–102, 114, 116–118
intervention and, 33–34, 99
and parent and professional relationships, 77, 84
Parenting Program and, 39–40, 44
and perpetuation of child maltreatment, 53
poverty and, 58
and preventing child maltreatment, 92–93
study methods and, 147, 153–154
Gil, D., 6, 71
Giovannoni, J., 4–6
Glaser, B., 145
Goffman, E., 138
Goldwyn, R., 54
Greenstein, R., 59–60
Gross, R., 133

Hall, N., 5, 54, 70
Helfer, R., 120
Henderson, C. R., 37
Hillam, 56

Intervention and interventionists, 122–123
and acquiring parenting skills, 96
active problem solving, 72
behavioral, 39–41
and changing system, 119, 121, 123, 131, 134
in contexts of family and community, 98–100
and empowering parents, 86–88
foster care. *See* Foster care and foster parents
and getting out of system, 102–107, 113–114, 116, 118
homemaker services, 68–69
legal. *See* Legal intervention
and parent and professional relationships, 81, 85–86
and Parenting Program, 39–46, 49
and preventing maltreatment, 91–92
service contracts, 66–67, 81, 85, 103
and study methods, 151
therapeutic, 70–73
Interviews
as method of obtaining information for study, 140–144
of parents, 10–30, 32–36, 47–48, 50, 66, 78–84, 96–98, 141–144

of staff members, 10–13, 25–26, 33, 39–41, 61–62, 64–65, 75–77
Isabelle (program co-director)
and acquiring parenting skills, 95–97
child's best interest and, 63–64
CPS and, 70
and empowering parents, 91
and getting out of system, 102–103
intervention and, 99
and parent and professional relationships, 75–76, 84–85
and preventing maltreatment, 92–93
and substantiating child abuse, 33

James, 56
Janko, Susan, 144
Jean (parent), 73
abused as child, 26–27
and acquiring parenting skills, 94, 96–97
and changing system, 125–126, 135–136
child's best interest and, 63
CPS and, 70, 72
and empowering parents, 88
family history of, 26–27, 50–52, 55
and getting out of system, 103, 106, 108, 114–116
legal intervention and, 34, 36
Parenting Program and, 44, 48–49
and perpetuation of child maltreatment, 50–52
poverty and, 56–58
and preventing maltreatment, 91
professional relationships and, 77
story of, 15–18
study methods and, 140, 142, 148, 153–155
Johnson, J. M., 155–156

Kaplan, J., 124
Kaufman, J., 50
Kazdin, A. E., 145
Kelly, W., 124
Kempe, C. H., 5, 71, 120
Kempe, R., 71
Kozol, Jonathan, 125, 127
Kuhn, Thomas, 125

Legal intervention, 33–37, 105
foster care and, 34–36
Parenting Program and, 33–34, 37, 39
and preventing maltreatment, 91
and social construction of child abuse, 4–5
Lightfoot, S. H., 137

McCrea, 4
Madsen, R., 121
Main, M., 54
Maria (parent), 78–81
Mayor's Task Force on Child Abuse and
    Neglect, 62
Meier, J. H., 2–3, 55, 71–72, 104
Merriam, S., 142
Methods of obtaining information, 9–13,
    137–156
    and adopting role of researcher, 152–156
    enumeration and sampling in, 144–145
    field study approach in, 138–145
    grounded theory approach in, 145–147
    interviews in, 140–144
    participant observations in, 139–140
    and quality assurance in qualitative re-
        search, 148–152
Minuchin, Salvador, 55, 120
Moynihan, D. P., 6
Musick, J., 72, 117, 119

Naylor, A., 133
Newberger, C. M., 72

Offord, D. R., 130
Olds, David, 72, 117, 119
Olds, G., 37
Orwell, G., 123

Palfrey, J., 129
Parenting Program, 7–10, 13–14, 31, 37–49
    and changing system, 118–120
    child's best interest and, 61–64, 66
    didactic training from, 39–40, 48
    and empowering parents, 86–91
    food served at, 43, 45–46
    and getting out of system, 101–104,
        106–107, 110–118
    interventions and, 33–34, 37, 39–46, 49,
        99–100
    lab school of, 40–41, 43–46
    location of, 42–43
    and parent and professional relation-
        ships, 75–76, 78, 83–86
    parents' impressions of, 47–49
    parents' stories and, 14, 19, 22, 25
    and perpetuation of child maltreatment,
        52
    poverty and, 41–42, 56, 59–61
    and preventing child maltreatment, 37–
        42, 91–93

and providing parenting knowledge and
    skills, 93, 95–98
service contracts and, 67–68
study methods and, 144–146, 153
Parents, 7–31, 66–91. *See also specific par-
    ents*
    abused as children, 7, 26–28, 30, 50, 73,
        100, 105, 115, 155
    in acquiring parenting knowledge and
        skills, 93–98
    and changing system, 119–121, 123–
        127, 129–136
    characteristics of, 2–3, 10
    child abuse perspectives of, 7–9
    child's best interest and, 62–66
    CPS and, 8, 66–73
    demographics of, 10
    doubting honesty of, 84
    earnestness of, 106–108
    family histories of, 25–30, 50–52, 54–56,
        59
    feelings of hopelessness experienced by,
        114–115
    and getting out of system, 101–118
    intervention and, 33–36, 96, 98–100
    interviews of, 10–30, 32–36, 47–48, 50,
        66, 78–84, 96–98, 141–144
    mental health of, 78–82
    Parenting Program and, 37–49
    as perpetrators of maltreatment, 25
    and perpetuation of child maltreatment,
        50–54
    poverty and, 7–8, 56–61
    and preventing child maltreatment, 91–
        92
    professional relationships and, 75–86
    service contracts and, 67–68
    and social construction of child abuse, 4
    stories of, 14–25
    study methods and, 9–10, 137–156
    substantiating child abuse and, 32–33
    supporting families by empowering, 86–
        91
    synergetic relationship between develop-
        ing children and, 3
Patterson, 39
Patton, M. Q., 141
Pauline (parent), 73
    abused as child, 30
    and acquiring parenting skills, 94, 97
    and changing system, 125–126, 135–
        136

court appearance of, 24
CPS and, 68–71
and empowering parents, 86, 88–89
family history of, 29–30, 55–56
and getting out of system, 101, 106–108, 114–117
intervention and, 34, 36, 99
Parenting Program and, 48–49
and perpetuation of child maltreatment, 52–54
poverty and, 56
and preventing maltreatment, 91–92
professional relationships and, 81–84
story of, 22–25
study methods and, 141, 147
Pazder, L., 1
Pelton, L. H., 2, 4–6, 56, 66
Peshkin, A., 149
Pianta, Robert, 2, 56, 59, 129–131
Porter, A., 60
Poverty, 121, 147
    categories of people in, 127
    as cause of child maltreatment, 55–61
    and changing system, 123–127, 129–130, 132
    children in, 12, 55–61
    and getting out of system, 105, 107, 114
    Parenting Program and, 41–42, 56, 59–61
    parents and, 7–8, 56–61
    service contracts and, 67
    and social construction of child abuse, 5–6
Provence, S., 133

Ramey, C., 133
Reiss, D., 54–55
Rescorla, L., 133
Risk, 128–130
Rizley, R., 55
Rutter, M., 54

Sameroff, Arnold, 2, 39, 73, 125
Schwendiman, M., 60
Shapiro, I., 59–60
Shinn, E., 65
Sia, C. J., 130
Silver, H. K., 5
Silverman, F., 5
Simeonsson, R., 130
Singer, J., 129

Skinner, B. F., 39
Skrtic, T., 125
Sloan, M. P., 2–3, 55, 71–72, 104
Smith, M., 1
Sparling, J., 133
Speiker, D., 133
Spradley, J. P., 153
Sroufe, L., 59
Staff members, 74, 114–115
    and acquiring parenting skills, 95
    and changing system, 118–120
    child's best interest and, 61–66
    and empowering parents, 86
    and getting out of system, 102–103, 107, 110, 113–115
    interviews of, 10–13, 25–26, 33, 39–41, 61–62, 64–65, 75–77
    legal intervention and, 33–34, 36
    and parent and professional relationships, 75–83, 85–86
    Parenting Program and, 39–40, 42–46, 48
    and perpetuation of child maltreatment, 52
    study methods and, 137–141, 145, 150, 153–154
    substantiating child abuse and, 33
Steele, B., 5
Strauss, A., 145
Strauss, M. A., 1
Sullivan, K., 144
Sullivan, W. M., 121
Suzuki, S., 124–125
Swidler, A., 121

Taylor, S. J., 141, 153
Tipton, S. M., 121
Tjossem, T., 128, 131
Tonge, 56
Trivette, 39

Van Maanen, J., 153
Veltman, M., 144
Vondra, J., 2

Walker, D., 129
Wasik, B., 133
Wolcott, Harry, 139, 148–152
Wolfe, D., 2
Woodward, J. K., 1

Zelditch, M., 138–140, 144
Zigler, Edward, 5, 50, 54, 70, 125, 132

ABOUT THE AUTHOR

Susan Janko is Associate Director of the University Affiliated Program at the Child Development and Mental Retardation Center, University of Washington. Her professional interests are in the areas of early child development and the influence of policies, service systems, and the social ecology on children and families.